COLORADO FRONT RANGE
Scenic & Historic Byways

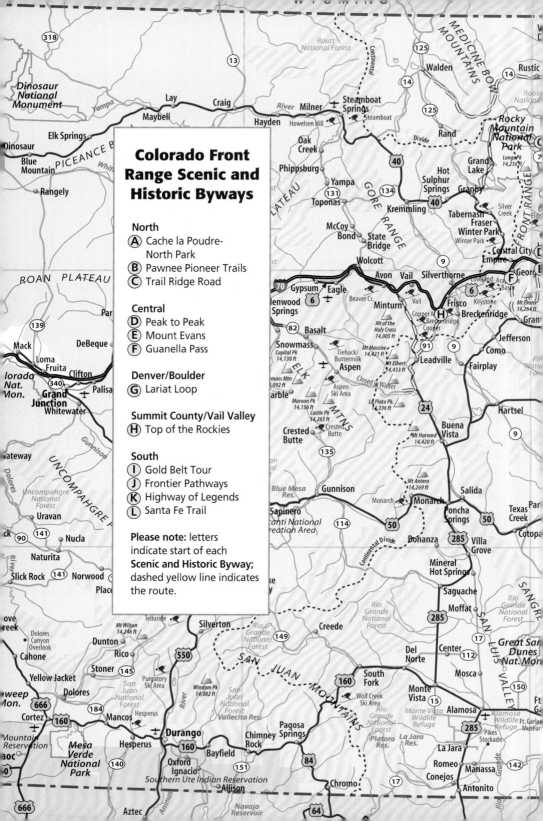

COLORADO FRONT RANGE
Scenic & Historic Byways

by Nancy and David Muenker

Publication Information

Altitude Publishing Ltd.
1500 Railway Avenue
Canmore, Alberta T1W 1P6
www.altitudepublishing.com

Cataloging in Publication Data

Muenker, Nancy, 1948-
Colorado Front Range scenic and historic byways /
Nancy and David Muenker.

(An Altitude superguide)
Includes index.
ISBN 1-55265-054-5

1. Automobile travel--Front Range (Colo. and Wyo.)--Guidebooks. 2. Historic sites--Front Range (Colo. and Wyo.)--Guidebooks. 3. Front Range (Colo. and Wyo.)--Guidebooks. I. Muenker, David, 1952- II. Title. III. Series: Altitude superguide.
F782.F88M842 2003   978.8'6   C2003-910889-9

Printed and bound in Canada by Friesen Printers

Altitude GreenTree Program

Altitude Publishing will plant twice as many trees as were used in the manufacturing of this product.

Project Development

Design/Layout	Stephen Hutchings
Maps	Hermien Schuttenbeld
	Mark Higenbottam
	Scott Manktelow

Note from the Publisher

The world described in *Altitude SuperGuides* is a unique and fascinating place. It is a world filled with surprise and discovery, beauty and enjoyment, questions and answers. It is a world of people, cities, landscape, animals and wilderness as seen through the eyes of those who live in, work with, and care for this world. The process of describing this world is also a means of defining ourselves.

It is also a world of relationship, where people derive their meaning from a deep and abiding contact with the land—as well as from each other. And it is this sense of relationship that guides all of us at Altitude to ensure that these places continue to survive and evolve in the decades ahead.

Altitude SuperGuides are books intended to be used, as much as read. Like the world they describe, Altitude SuperGuides are evolving, adapting and growing. Please write to us with your comments and observations, and we will do our best to incorporate your ideas into future editions of these books.

Stephen Hutchings
Publisher

Front cover: Phantom Canyon Road on Gold Belt Tour
Back cover: Gold mine ruins near Victor
Title page: Sangre de Cristo Range and Wet Mountain Valley
Opposite: Mine ruins in Vindicator Valley

Introduction

I n every direction, Colorado displays priceless sights. They may be as breathtaking as the snow-capped Sangre de Cristo Mountains glistening at sunrise, as endearing as newborn elk grazing on the tundra in Rocky Mountain National Park, or as uplifting as an eagle soaring above Pawnee Buttes.

Scores of highways and back roads lace the state's mountains and plains. Among these, 24 have been designated Colorado Scenic and Historic Byways. To gain byway designation, a route must possess a variety of extraordinary features and experiences for the traveler, such as historical sites, wildlife, educational opportunities and recreation.

Twelve of the state designated byways fall within the geographic scope of this book. While exploring them, travelers traverse prairies, wind through foothills and canyons and scale mountain slopes. Elevations range from 4,000 feet on the plains to 14,264 feet atop Mount Evans.

These landscapes yield such ancient treasures as dinosaur tracks, petroglyphs and petrified sequoias. Volcanic plugs, finlike dikes, sandstone towers and other bizarre formations tease the imagination.

Wildlife viewing and bird watching opportunities abound. Wild turkeys scurry through prairie sagebrush while moose nibble on willow bushes in montane meadows and Rocky Mountain bighorn sheep bound up alpine slopes.

Throughout the summer, wildflowers beautify grasslands, meadows and tundra. In autumn, aspens streak forests with golden hues stippled red and orange. Winter snows dust canyon walls and turn peaks into shimmering diamonds.

Amid the natural wonders, travelers can enjoy numerous recreational activities, from fishing in a mountain stream to climbing the final ascent of a fourteener. Other options include hiking, rafting, rock climbing, mountain biking,

Opposite: Geneva Creek
Above: Sagebrush carpets North Park

skiing and snowshoeing, to name a few.

The Front Range's history surfaces along the byways. Some of the roads retrace former Indian, fur trapper and goldseeker trails. Others parallel bygone stagecoach, wagon and rail routes. Through museums and restored districts, towns evoke their colorful heritages as agricultural colonies, railroad hubs and mining camps.

Each byway showcases a unique blend of wildlife, vegetation, geology, history, cultural heritage and recreation. Moreover, each season – indeed, each trip – presents a different experience.

Explore and enjoy these byways many times.

History of the Colorado Scenic and Historic Byways Program

The Colorado Scenic and Historic Byways program was officially established in 1989 to showcase outstanding examples of the state's scenery and heritage. Local partnership groups nominate byways for potential designation by the Colorado Scenic and Historic Byways Commission. To be designated, a proposed byway must possess unusual, exceptional and/or distinctive scenic, historical, cultural, wildlife, recreational, educational, geological or natural features. Other key criteria are strong local support and commitment to develop and promote tourism.

In its first year, the program designated five routes. Among them were three Front Range byways: Peak to Peak Highway, Highway of Legends and Gold Belt Tour. By 1994, the state had 21 byways. Two more were added in 1998 and 1999 respectively. The Lariat Loop, unique in its proximity to a major metropolitan area, joined the select group in August 2002. At that time, the commission also approved the addition of Cordova Pass Road to the Highway of Legends.

Currently, 24 Colorado Scenic and Historic Byways lead travelers through distinctive landscapes etched with fascinating history. Blue roadside signs bearing the columbine, Colorado's state flower, mark each route.

Additional information about the routes, including the program's official booklet, Discover Colorado, can be obtained at state welcome centers, chambers of commerce, local visitor centers, National Forest Service offices and similar facilities. Many of the byways have created videos and printed brochures. The Colorado Scenic and Historic Byways program also maintains an official web site, http://coloradobyways.colorado.edu/main.cfm.

Life Zones

Life zones identify the distribution of plant and animal communities across landscapes. Factors that influence where specific plants grow or animals reside include climate, soil chemistry, topography and altitude. Colorado has five distinct life zones. Delineated by elevation, they are the plains, foothills, montane, subalpine and alpine zones. Timberline, the point at which trees stop growing, occurs between the subalpine and alpine life zones.

Plains Zone – 3,500 to 6,000 feet

A semi-arid grassland ecosystem characterizes much of Colorado's high plains. The Pawnee and Comanche Grasslands showcase the short-grass prairie that was common before settlement. Shrubs include rabbitbrush, snakeweed and sagebrush. Cottonwoods, willows and other

Photographs, left to right:
1. Plains zone
2. Foothills zone
3. Montane zone
4. Subalpine zone

trees grow only along streams and rivers. Among other plants are yucca, prickly pear cactus and evening primrose. Common animals include prairie dogs, jackrabbits, coyotes, deer and pronghorn antelope. Among the hundreds of feathered species are mountain plover, prairie falcons and ferruginous hawks.

Foothills Zone – 6,000 to 8,000 feet

Typically carpeted with scrub oak and piñon-juniper woodlands, this zone's high rolling hills separate the plains from the mountains. At higher elevations, ponderosa pines, Douglas firs, blue spruces and aspens also grow. A diverse variety of wildflowers speckles the landscape. Red-tailed hawks, wild turkeys and golden eagles are frequently seen. Common animals include red foxes, raccoons and mountain lions.

Montane Zone – 8,000 to 10,000 feet

Thick forests and vast mountain meadows define this zone. Aspen groves lace stands of lodgepoles, limber pines, Douglas firs and blue spruce. Wild rose, Oregon grape and pasque flowers brighten the understory. Tassel-eared Abert squirrels nibble on ponderosa pine cones. Other animals include mule deer, cottontail rabbits and bighorn sheep. A profusion of wild iris, shooting stars and other wildflowers dapple grassy meadows. Great horned owls, magpies, and mountain chickadees count among the bird population.

10

Subalpine Zone – 10,000–11,500 feet

Dense forests of Englemann spruce and sub-alpine fir blanket slopes. Ancient bristlecone pines cling to Mount Evans. Clark's nutcrackers, Stellar's jays and blue grouse are among this zone's common bird inhabitants. Bluebells, columbines and kinnikinnik accent the terrain. Elk, pine martins, black bears and snowshoe hares populate the area.

Timberline – About 11,500 feet

Krummholz, German for "crooked wood," signals the transition from forests to tundra. Harsh, dessicating winds and extreme weather stunt and twist Engelmann spruce, subalpine fir and bristlecone pine trees into grotesque shapes. Above timberline, trees no longer grow.

Alpine Zone – 11,500 and higher

Mosses, lichens, cushion plants and various sedges and grasses hug the treeless, windswept tundra. Delicate, yet hardy, Old Man of the Mountain, alpine phlox and numerous other wildflowers cling to the terrain. Pika, chipmunks and yellow-bellied marmots inhabit rocky areas. Elk summer at this high elevation.

Colorado State Symbols

Animal: Rocky Mountain Bighorn Sheep
Found only in the Rockies, bighorn sheep boast massive horns which curve backward from the forehead, down, then forward.

Bird: Lark Bunting
The male bird of this migrant species performs a spectacular courtship flight, during which it warbles and trills a distinctive mating song.

Fish: Greenback Cutthroat Trout
Efforts to protect and propagate this colorful fish have brought it back from near extinction.

Flower: The white and lavender Columbine
The state song, "Where the Columbines Grow," reveres this rare species.

Fossil: Stegosaurus
In 1877 a significant dinosaur quarry was discovered near Cañon City, yielding some of the most complete skeletons ever exhumed, including a stegosaurus skeleton now housed in the Denver Museum of Nature and Science.

Gem: Aquamarine
Crystals extracted from Mount Antero and White Mountain range in color from light blue to deep aquamarine green and measure up to 6 centimeters long.

Grass: Blue Grama
Growing throughout several life zones, this Colorado native enhances soil conservation.

Insect: Colorado Hairstreak Butterfly
Purple wings with black borders and orange accents mark this colorful inhabitant of scrub oak ecosystems.

Tree: Colorado Blue Spruce
A distinctive silver-blue color and symmetrical shape distinguish this majestic tree, first discovered on Pikes Peak in 1862.

Photographs this page:
1. Timberline region
2. Alpine zone

Opposite page: Mountain goat

Cache la Poudre-North Park

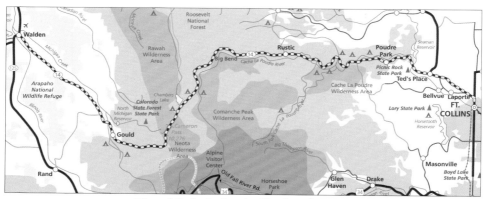

Map of Cache La Poudre-North Park Byway

Wild waters froth as they roar through sheer-walled Poudre Canyon. Beyond a range of craggy peaks, moose nibble wetland willows and songbirds trill. Along the Cache la Poudre-North Park Byway, sights and sounds vary from wild to serene.

The route courses westward from Fort Collins to Walden, following the Cache la Poudre River, then climbing over Cameron Pass into mountain-rimmed North Park.

As it leaves Fort Collins, the 101-mile byway passes ranches and irrigated farms, reminders of the town's origin as an agricultural colony. Paralleling Cache la Poudre River, it enters Poudre Canyon. The river's French name means "hiding place for powder." According to lore, French fur trappers caught in a blizzard lightened their load by burying boxes of gunpowder (poudre) in a hiding place (cache) along the riverbank.

The canyon walls squeeze the valley into a tight corridor, the Narrows. Sides of sheer granite soar to heights of 3,000 feet. The river growls as it scours bedrock and careens around sharp bends.

Farther up the road, the canyon widens. The Cache la Poudre River's outstanding scenery, recreation and water quality earned it designation as a national Wild and Scenic River. These qualities lure rafters, kayakers and anglers to its waters.

At Mountain Park Recreation Area, one of many roadside day use sites, travelers can picnic riverside under ponderosa pines. In a kids' fishing hole, youngsters can try to catch trout. Interpretive panels help them identify the types they reel in.

After passing the town of Rustic, the byway reaches Arrowhead Lodge Visitor Center, run by the National Forest Service. Inside the former mountain resort's log structure, one of the exhibits displays vials containing trout at various stages of growth, from zak fry to adults. Outside, visitors can peer into rustic 1930s cabins and an ice house that once held 25 tons of ice cut from the river—enough for the former resort's summer needs.

A short distance beyond, the State Trout Rearing Unit borders the river. Since the ponds have been drained due to whirling disease, the facility's trout are now raised in raceways. Visitors are welcome to feed the fish with site-provided food.

The canyon floor broadens at Big Bend, known for its bighorn sheep viewing area. Travelers often spot them on the steep northern slope.

As the byway climbs in elevation, stands of pine and aspen cover the hillsides. Spray spews above the river where Poudre Falls cascades 100 feet. Its turbulent tumble awes those who descend the slope for better viewing.

Near Chambers Lake, the Cache la Poudre River veers south while the byway continues west to North Park. The jagged silhouette of Nokhu Crags heralds the ascent of Cameron Pass. Cresting at 10,276 feet, the road descends into the thick lodgepole woodlands of Colorado State Forest, the state's largest park.

About five miles beyond the pass, Moose Visitor Center educates travelers about the park's wildlife, especially its prized animal, the moose. Crowned with massive palmate antlers, a stuffed specimen stands 6 feet high in the middle of the exhibit room. A distinctive fold of skin, called a dewlap, dangles from its throat. Visitors can listen to recorded moose sounds, stroke bristly hide and learn about the animal's fondness for willows, water lilies and other riparian plants.

The byway parallels Michigan River, which meanders through bogs, wet meadows and willow thickets — prime moose habitat. Not native to Colorado, the largest of the deer species was introduced into the area in the late 1970s and

Photographs, left to right:
1. Motorcyclists enter the Narrows.
2. Autumn along the Cache la Poudre River
3. Rafters ride the rapids.
4. Craggy cliffs soar above the river.

now numbers about 500. Travelers may spot these creatures anywhere along the byway from Chambers Lake to Walden.

As the road enters North Park, the terrain transforms from thick forest to low rolling hills carpeted with sagebrush. Towering ranges rim the expansive basin. During the time when large herds of wild buffalo grazed here, Ute Indians called it "Bull Pen." Cattle and hay fields now accent the landscape.

Three miles before the byway's western point, the road borders the Arapaho National Wildlife Refuge, where waterfowl and other migratory birds can nest and rear their young. The best time to observe birds is may through October.

A ridge-top overlook captures a view of the Illinois River below, squiggling southward through wetlands. Although the refuge is accessible from the byway via a county road, easier entries turn off Colorado 125, just south of the ranching community of Walden. Along a nature trail, white-tailed jackrabbits hop among shrubs while yellow warblers fill the air with song. As travelers drive the self-guided auto route, pronghorns graze in sagebrush flats bordering ponds that sustain gadwalls, American avocet and other waterfowl.

From Cache la Poudre River's thundering waters and steep canyon walls to North Park's huge moose and sweet birdsongs, the byway presents a wondrous show of sight and sound.

Ducks and More Galore

Using water from the Illinois River, the Arapaho National Wildlife Refuge irrigates meadows and maintains waterfowl brood ponds that annually produce some 400 goslings and 8,000 ducklings. The refuge also attracts dozens of other species of shore and wading birds. Among them are American avocets, white-faced ibis and black-crowned night herons. The area supports diverse wildlife habitat including wetlands, sagebrush-grassland uplands, and mixed conifer and aspen woodlands. Atop an escarpment which County Road 32 parallels, the Illinois River Overlook captures a panorama of the expansive refuge. Visitors can explore the area

both on foot and via car. The half-mile Interpretive Nature Trail, accessed from Colorado 125, passes through wetlands and mudflats. A symphony of bird song fills the air. Beavers and muskrats swim in the meandering river while American white pelicans fly overhead in V formation. The self-guided auto tour, also off Colorado 125 (brochures at the entrance kiosk), traverses sagebrush flats, a prime habitat for sage grouse and pronghorns, as it winds around water impoundments. Travelers may spot golden eagles, prairie falcons and other raptors circling overhead. Small, shallow ponds rich with insects and other invertebrates nurture the breeding and feeding of waterfowl. Tall, dense grasses harbor duck nests. Islands and over-the-water platforms provide geese with nesting areas safe from raccoons and other predators. The best months for observing birds are May through October. The peak migration occurs in late May when 5,000 or more ducks may be present. [Main entrance and headquarters off Colorado 125, 8 miles south of Walden; 970-723-8202; free; open year-round.]

Photographs, left to right:
1. Cache la Poudre is Colorado's only Wild and Scenic River.
2. Poudre Falls cascades 100 feet.
3. Nokhu Crags scrape the sky.
4. Medicine Bow Mountains rise east of North Park.

Towering Twig Eaters

Camouflaged by willow bushes, moose feed on tender twigs and buds, endorsing their Algonquin Indian name, "eater of twigs." These long-legged creatures are the largest members of the deer family. Bulls reach a shoulder height of 6 1/2 to 7 1/2 feet and weigh from 800 to 1600 pounds. Their distinctive antlers are flat and palmate, with points forming only at the edges. A mature male's rack can measure five feet across and weigh 80 pounds. In comparison, cows have no antlers, reach shoulder heights of 5 to 6 1/2 feet and weigh 600 to 1,000 pounds. A shoulder hump, blunt muzzle, and dewlap, or fold of skin dangling from the throat, characterize both sexes.

Moose were first introduced into Colorado in 1978 and 1979 in North Park. They adapted well to the chosen habitat of willows and lodgepole pines at 9,000 feet. Another group was released in 1987 into Laramie River drainage off Cameron Pass. From the initial 36 moose, the herd now numbers about 500. They have migrated to Kawuneeche Valley and other locations in Rocky Mountain National Park west of the Continental Divide, Middle Park and upper reaches of the Cache la Poudre River. The Colorado Division of Wildlife released additional moose in the early 1990s northwest of Creede. Today the statewide population of twig eaters has reached about 1,000. Early mornings and early evenings are the best times to look for moose, but they may be seen throughout the day, especially along streams and ponds.

Wild and Scenic River

In 1968, the U.S. Congress enacted landmark legislation, the Wild and Scenic Rivers Act, which recognized the need to balance a policy of damming and diverting rivers with one of maintaining other rivers in a free-flowing condition. To be designated a Wild and Scenic River, a river or part thereof must be free-flowing and have at least one "outstandingly remarkable value," such as scenery, recreation or water quality. The Cache la Poudre, Colorado's only Wild and Scenic River, boasts all three. This designation means that no new dams or diversions will be built on the Cache la Poudre within the 75 miles included under the act. Future water development can, however, be considered along any other portion of the river.

Fort Collins

Fort Collins straddles the Cache la Poudre River in the middle of rich agricultural country. Students of Colorado State University infuse the city with youthful enthusiasm. Renovated in the 1980s, Old Town has trendy shops, restaurants and a sculpture-studded plaza. Several pubs craft distinctive microbrews.

History buffs can explore the town's lore and origins at the Fort Collins Museum and Avery House. The Farm at Lee Martinez Park acquaints both young and old with animals and agriculture. Cottonwoods and willows shade walkers as they stroll alongside the Cache la Poudre River. Canada geese, beavers and great blue herons are some of the species that inhabit this riparian area. Horsetooth Reservoir attracts anglers, boaters and windsurfers. Numerous hiking and biking paths thread through the city and neighboring parks. In addition, prime rafting and kayaking locations are just a few miles up the byway in Poudre Canyon.

Photographs this page:
1. The Illinois River winds through Arapaho National Wildlife Refuge.
2. Nokhu Crags and Lake Agnes

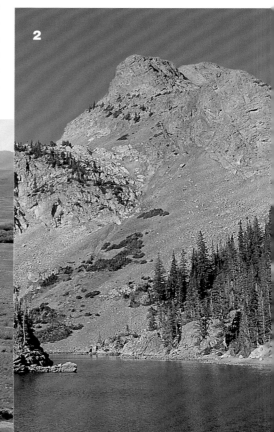

Pawnee Pioneer Trails

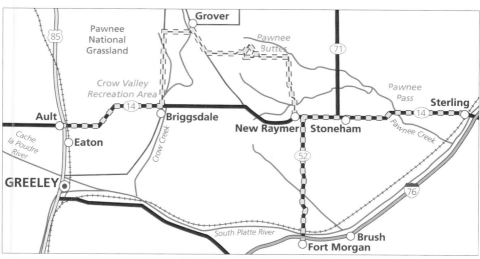

Map of Pawnee Pioneer Trails Byway

On the high plains of northeastern Colorado, the Pawnee Buttes jut skyward, creating a distinctive landmark for travelers and a nesting site for raptors. The songs of longspurs, mountain plovers, and hundreds of other migratory birds carry on the prairie wind.

Paralleling both migratory bird flyways and historic human pathways, the Pawnee Pioneer Trails byway stretches from Ault to Sterling. In this region, traders trod along Trappers Trail, goldseekers and pioneers gouged ruts into the Overland Trail, and Texas longhorn cattle thundered on the Goodnight-Loving Trail.

The 128-mile route starts north of Greeley in Ault, a town developed as a siding along the Union Pacific Railroad. Tall grain elevators symbolize its agricultural economy. As it follows Colorado 14 east, the byway passes fence posts topped with boots, sneakers and other discarded footwear. Evergreen trees form a "living snowfence." Grand vistas of gently undulating plains stretch to the distant horizon.

Within 10 miles, the route begins passing through sections of Pawnee National Grassland, which are interspersed with farms and ranches.

Photographs this page:
1. Yuccas blossom amid native grasses on Pawnee Grassland.
2. Moonrise over the Pawnee Buttes

Trip Planner: Pawnee Pioneer Trails

Route: Follows Colorado 14 east from Ault to Briggsdale, north on Country Road 77 and east on County Road 120 to Grover, southeast on County Road 390 and east on County Road 112 to the Pawnee Buttes, east on County Road 110 and south on County Roads 127 and 129 to Raymer, and east on Colorado 14 to Sterling. A spur leads south on Colorado 52 to Fort Morgan.

Total length: 128 miles.

Driving time: Three hours excluding stops.

Outstanding features: Pawnee Buttes, Pawnee National Grassland, prairie ecosystem.

Vehicle restrictions: None.

Accessibility: Year-round.

Special considerations: Gravel roads. Avoid in heavy rain or snow. Be alert to livestock on road in open range areas.

Key events: Grover Rodeo, Grover, Father's Day weekend; Potato Day, Greeley, second Saturday of September; Sugar Beet Days and Oktoberfest, Sterling, third weekend of September.

Contact: USFS-Pawnee National Grassland, 970-353-5004. Greeley Convention & Visitors Bureau, 800-449-3866, 970-352-3566, www.greeleycvb.com; Logan County Chamber of Commerce, 866-522-5070, www.logancountychamber.com.

The short-grass prairie habitat sustains pronghorns, swift foxes and hundreds of other animals as well as nearly 300 birds.

At Briggsdale, the byway heads north on County Road 77. Here, Crow Valley Recreation Area entices travelers with a picnic area shaded by towering cottonwoods, an outdoor museum displaying plows and other farm equipment, and a trail into a wildlife area.

This juncture is also the starting point for a side trip — a self-guided birding tour by car or mountain bike through the northwest sections of the grassland. Birdwatchers may see loggerhead shrikes, American kestrels and Colorado's state bird, the lark bunting. Numerous birds can also be spotted along the byway, especially on telephone wires and fence posts.

When the route turns east toward Grover, a hazy silhouette of the Chalk Bluffs rises into view. Horses and cattle graze on ranchlands. Farms grow corn, wheat and hay. Some do dry land cultivation while others do either flood or sprinkler irrigation.

At Grover, the road heads southeast. Like several of the byway towns, its location on the Sterling-Cheyenne branch of the Chicago, Burlington and Quincy Railroad, aka the "Prairie Dog Special," attracted early homesteaders. The railroad not only shipped their livestock, cream, eggs and grain to market but also brought them coal, lumber and merchandise.

The Grover Depot Museum chronicles the railroad years through memorabilia, photographs and artifacts. Painted bright red with teal trim, the two-story building also houses the station master's upstairs quarters.

Derricks and horses share the surrounding ranchlands. The byway then turns east toward the Pawnee Buttes. A scenic overlook frames a view of the 250-foot-high landmarks. To fully appreciate their scale and the surrounding habitat, travelers can hike a 1.5-mile trail to the base of the west butte. (The east butte is

privately owned.) The area attracts birds of prey, including golden eagles, ferruginous hawks and prairie falcons. Access to the cliffs near the buttes is closed March through June to protect nesting raptors.

East of the buttes, the road turns south, following a straight ribbon of gravel over rolling terrain and past rock outcroppings. A "forest" of yucca plants carpets the landscape. At Raymer, travelers can choose to turn east on Colorado 14 to the byway's eastern terminus in Sterling or follow a segment south on Colorado 52 to Fort Morgan.

When it served as a military post, Fort Morgan protected telegraph lines, mail routes and Overland Trail travelers. Today, an exquisite rainbow arch bridge, aptly named Rainbow Bridge and listed on the National Register of Historic Places, spans the South Platte River. Exhibits in the Fort Morgan Museum honor the town's most illustrious citizen, 1930s Big Band leader Glenn Miller.

Back on Colorado 14, the byway stretches across the plains to Sterling. The Overland Trail brought homesteaders hailing from Tennessee and Mississippi to this region in the 1870s. The town became incorporated shortly after the Union Pacific and Burlington railroads created a junction there.

Housed in a replica of a fort, the Overland Trail Museum relates the history of northeastern Colorado. Exhibits describe the trail to western gold fields and the enormous ranching empires developed by John Wesley Iliff and other cattle barons. The museum's impressive collections include saddles, branding irons and antique toys. Outside, visitors can step into a huge red barn, small church, barber shop and other historic buildings filled with period items.

Revival of the Prairie

National grasslands were born of the dual tragedy of the 1930s Dust Bowl and Great Depression. During the severe drought, scouring winds lifted top soil from plowed fields into dust clouds that rose more than 20,000 feet. The federal government purchased the devastated lands from farmers and helped resettle destitute families. Windbreaks, erosion control devices and the planting of grasses helped rehabilitate the worn-out prairie. In 1960, these federally-owned tracts became the National Grasslands. Two of them, Comanche National Grassland (see page 60) and Pawnee National Grassland, are located in Colorado. The U.S. Forest Service manages them for cattle grazing, limited oil extraction, plant and wildlife habitat, and recreation. Blue grama, buffalo grasses and other perennial prairie grasses continue to stabilize the soil by reducing water and wind erosion. Sections of the Pawnee Grassland lie intermingled with private properties over a 30-by-60 mile area in northeast Colorado, roughly bounded east-west by Colorado 71 and U.S. 85, and north-south by the state border and Colorado 14. From the flat, expansive prairie, the Pawnee Buttes rise some 250 feet high. Open

Photographs, left to right:
1. Pawnee Buttes are a raptor nesting area.
2. Windmill powers a cattle ranch's water pump.
3. Red barn at Overland Trail Museum
4. American white pelicans summer at North Sterling Reservoir.

plains, woody draws, cliffs, tree-lined creek bottoms and springs characterize the Pawnee Grassland. These habitats sustain coyotes, pronghorn antelope, mule deer, swift foxes, and prairie dogs. They also attract more than 300 species of birds, including Colorado's state bird, the lark bunting. A 36-mile self-guided birding tour, suitable for vehicles and mountain bikes, passes through a variety of bird habitats. Along the Pawnee Buttes Trail (cliff access closed during the raptor nesting season, March 1 through June 30), hikers can admire the prairie environment, from colorful prickly pear cactus to soaring red-tailed hawks. [Pawnee National Grassland, 660 "O" Street, Greeley, CO; 303-353-5004]

The Visiting Big Bird

Like annual vacationers, thousands of American white pelicans flock every summer to eastern Colorado's ponds and reservoirs. These huge birds can measure more than five feet long and have up to nine-foot wing spans. Black wing tips, yellow bills and orange feet accent their brilliant white bodies. Airborne, they double their necks back against their shoulders, which helps distinguish them from other birds in flight. To feed, they float on shallow water, swaying their bills side to side, scooping fish into their enormous pouches. When food is widely dispersed, the pelicans form a semi-circle and "herd" prey toward shore. When they take flight, they soar to great heights, with their brilliant white bodies shimmering in the sky like mirrors.

Photographs this page:
1. Cottonwoods shade Crow Valley Recreation Area.
2. Rainbow Bridge spans South Platte River.

Greeley

Established as the Union Colony of Colorado in 1870, Greeley brought the first agricultural colonists to the region's high plains. Members received rail transportation west and the chance to buy residential lots and farmland with water rights. Through perseverance and effective irrigation methods, the settlement thrived. The state granted Greeley the first Normal School of Colorado, now the University of Northern Colorado. Sugar beet production, ranching and beef processing became prominent industries. Locals annually celebrate their heritage with a grand rodeo, the Greeley Independence Stampede.

The abundant flowers and trees in the George M. Houston Gardens would have dazzled the Union Colonists. The educational nature center displays indigenous plants of Colorado's various life zones, shortening the distance from the plains to timberline into a leisurely walk. Several Greeley sites relate the region's history. The houses in Centennial Village Museum depict the lifestyles of different eras and ethnic groups. At Meeker House Museum, guides relate the life and times of the Union Colony founder, Nathan Meeker.

Trail Ridge Road

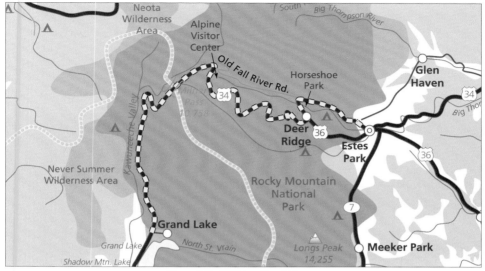

Map of Trail Ridge Road Byway

Brisk winds push dark thunder clouds up a glaciated valley. In an alpine meadow carpeted with lush grasses, newborn white-spotted elk frolic under the watchful eyes of their mothers. Around another bend, the snow-mantled Never Summer Mountains gleam like pearls.

Such dramatic sights unfold as Trail Ridge Road traverses Rocky Mountain National Park between the towns of Estes Park and Grand Lake. The 48-mile byway climbs through three life zones—montane, subalpine and alpine—before reaching its highest point, 12,183 feet, and crossing the Continental Divide. Distinctive flora and fauna populate each of the zones.

From its east end, Estes Park, the road ascends through glades and grasslands into Horseshoe Park. During June and July, Rocky

Photographs this page:
1. Snow caps Mummy Range.
2. Fall River winds through Horseshoe Park.

Mountain bighorn sheep flock to Sheep Lakes, a natural mineral lick rich with nutrients. In midsummer, Indian paintbrush, golden aster and silvery lupine deck the meadows. Seeking food and warmer temperatures, elk gravitate here in autumn, making it a prime viewing area in the rutting season.

At the bend in Horseshoe Park, Old Fall River Road—the route that in 1920 opened the national park to automotive traffic—splits off the byway. Convicts labored seven years building it through steep, narrow canyons. For the adventurous, the 9-mile, one-way dirt road offers a gripping alternative route to Fall River Pass and the Alpine Visitor Center.

Trail Ridge Road continues westward on U.S. 34. Switchbacking upward, it reaches a subalpine ecosystem populated with Engelmann spruce and subalpine fir. The first scenic overlook, Many Parks Curve, captures a vista of glacier-carved valleys studded with lakes. Radiant as a diamond, Longs Peak soars 14,255 feet high. Each of the byway overlooks frames a unique panorama.

Near Rainbow Curve, the road reaches two miles above sea level. Trees begin to show the effects of the harsh environment. Fierce winds have sculpted firs into flag trees, whose branches grow only on the leeward side. Near 11,000 feet, trees stand only as high as the surrounding protective rocks, forming into dense, low growth called krummholz, a German word meaning crooked wood. Then, as if halting at a battle line etched in the granite, tree growth stops. There, the byway reaches timberline and the tundra.

Trip Planner: Trail Ridge Road

Route: Follows U.S. 34 between Rocky Mountain National Park's east entrance at Estes Park and its west entrance at Grand Lake.
Total length: 48 miles.
Driving time: Two hours one way, excluding stops.
Outstanding features: Exhilarating scenery, tundra and other high-altitude ecosystems, wildlife viewing, hiking.
Vehicle restrictions: None.
Accessibility: Open from about Memorial Day through mid-October, weather permitting. During other months, a few miles of road near each entrance can be driven.
Special considerations: No gas stations between park entrances. Weather can suddenly change. Elevation ranges from 8,000 feet to more than 12,000 feet.
Key events: Estes Park Wool Market, Estes Park, Father's Day weekend; High Altitude Sled Dog Championship, Grand Lake, last weekend of February.
Fee: National Park Service entrance fee.
Contact: Rocky Mountain National Park, 970-586-1206, www.nps.gov/romo. Chambers of Commerce: Estes Park, 800-443-7837, 70-586-4431, www.estesparkresort.com, and Grand Lake, 970-627-3402, www.grandlakechamber.com.

A short trail crosses the rugged, yet fragile, terrain to Forest Canyon Overlook. On the slope of Sundance Mountain rocks form patterns of precise circles, polygons and "streams" that flow downhill – all the result of the tundra freezing and thawing in the last Ice Age.

Rock Cut reveals one of the greatest challenges that construction crews faced when building Trail Ridge Road in the early 1930s. Carving the byway through solid layers of gneiss and schist took three summers. Even so, workers took special care to protect the landscape. They covered nearby rock outcroppings to avoid scarring during dynamite blasts, collected rubble and turned disturbed rocks lichen-side up.

Uphill from the cut, Tundra Communities Trail showcases a natural rock garden of delicate, miniature flowers. A 5-year-old plant may be no larger than a fingertip. Close inspection reveals the pink petals of moss campion, the deep blue blossoms of forget-me-nots and the brilliant yellow disks of alpine sunflowers.

Just before reaching the Alpine Visitor Center, the byway reaches its highest point, 12,183

Photographs, left to right:
1. Aspens turn radiant gold.
2. Alpine view of Longs Peak
3. Erosion sculpted these formations of granite capped with schist.
4. Water lilies dapple Bear Lake.

feet. With park exhibits, snack bar and gift shop, the center is a favorite rest stop. Nearby, Alpine Ridge Trail leads to vast, lofty views. Yellow-bellied marmots bask in the sun while squeaking pikas scurry among the rocks. Ptarmigans, the only birds that winter on the tundra, blend with the landscape. In summer, they sport mottled brown plumage while in the winter they are as white as the snow.

Always unpredictable, the weather can change at any moment. Temperatures may drop suddenly. Thunderstorms may roll in. Snow may fall, even in July.

As the byway begins its descent, the panorama sweeps north to Wyoming and west to the Gore Range. Herds of elk graze on steep grassy slopes stitched with pockets of snow. At Milner Pass (10,758 feet), travelers cross North America's watershed, the Continental Divide. Streams east of the divide flow into the Atlantic Ocean. Those to the west flow into the Pacific Ocean.

The road curves down through corridors of towering trees, then unveils vistas of the Kawuneeche Valley ribboned with the Colorado River. Sunbeams bounce off the snow-clad peaks aptly named Never Summer Mountains. From picnic areas, hiking trails lead into open meadows and cool forests. Gray jays flit among the trees. Mule deer may prong across the path. The sweet scent of vanilla welcomes those who sniff the sun-warmed bark of ponderosa pines.

At the site of Never Summer Ranch, guides relate stories about its attraction in the 1920s as a trout lodge. To the south, beaver dams obstruct gurgling streams. Camouflaged by

wetland willows, moose nibble tender twigs in the marshes. Elk often graze on the vast valley floor. During the autumn mating season, the bulls' eerie bugling pierces the air.

Trail Ridge Road ends at the west entrance of Rocky Mountain National Park near the resort village of Grand Lake. The byway's exhilarating grandeur changes with each turn, each day, and each season, encouraging travelers to return often.

Viewing North American Elk or Wapiti

More than 3,000 elk populate Rocky Mountain National Park in summer months. By July, alpine meadows along Trail Ridge Road turn into "nurseries" populated with cow elk and their white-spotted calves grazing on lush grasses. As with most wildlife viewing, the best time to see elk is in the early morning and evening. Their coats are creamy brown with a dark mane and an off-white rump patch. These regal animals stand 4 to 5 feet high at the shoulder, with males larger than females. The antlers of mature bulls weigh 25 or more pounds and measure 5 feet across. Blood vessels contained in a protective soft covering called "velvet" nourish the growing antlers. In late summer, bulls remove the velvet and buff the exposed surfaces by rubbing their antlers against trees and bushes. They shed their racks annually between January and April. In autumn, elk migrate to lower elevations. The prime places to view them during mating season are Moraine Park, Upper Beaver Meadows and Horseshoe Park on the east side and Kawuneeche Valley on the west side. Mature bull elk bugle an eerie call to attract cows and intimidate rivals for control of harems. This bugling communicates a bull's strength, size and vigor. The deep, resonant tone rises about three octaves to a high-pitched squeal before dropping to a series of grunts. In the rutting season, the park's elk-viewing sites are closed to off-trail travel from 5 p.m. to 7 a.m. Roadside viewing is permitted provided that visitors park in lots or designated roadside areas.

Headwaters of the Colorado River

The legendary Colorado River officially begins its 1,440-mile journey to the Pacific Ocean at La Poudre Pass, high in the Never Summer Mountains of Rocky Mountain National Park. On its descent, the trickling ribbon of water widens into a stream, meandering through mountain meadows and across arid mesas before it thunders with canyon-cutting power. Originally called the Grand River, it gained its current name in 1921 by a resolution of both houses of

the U.S. Congress. In the west, water is treasured like currency. As a result, the river's water has been allocated since 1922 by the Colorado River Compact. This agreement divides the states through which the river flows into the Upper Basin (Colorado, New Mexico, Utah, Wyoming) and the Lower Basin (Arizona, California, Nevada) and apportions 7.5 million acre feet of water per year to each basin. The Upper Basin states signed an accord in 1948 for allocating their share. Colorado receives 51.75%, Utah, 23%, Wyoming 14% and New Mexico 11.25%.

Alpine Flowers

A magical world of delicate plants survives above timberline in the tundra. The harsh environment at this lofty elevation above 11,500 feet prevents trees from growing. Alpine flowers, however, have evolved to withstand punishing winds, temperature extremes, scant soil, limited water and an annual growing season squeezed into about 40 frost-free days. They cope in a

number of ways. Most hug the ground, growing only a couple of inches high but anchored with extensive root systems. The red pigment of the blossoms on moss campion and rosy paintbrush acts as a sunscreen against ultra-violet rays. In addition, many tundra plants grow waxy or woolly leaves to help hold water.

Grand Lake

Hugging the shores of Colorado's largest natural lake, the village of Grand Lake brims with recreational activities. Water skiers, windsurfers, boaters and anglers share the shimmering waters of Grand Lake and Shadow Mountain Lake. All the wonders of Rocky Mountain National Park and other federal lands are mere minutes away. In winter, the town transforms into a snowmobiling hub, with access to more than 100 miles of groomed trails. Ice fishing sheds dot the lakes' flat, frozen expanse.

Before becoming a lakeside resort, the town served as a supply center for 19th-century prospectors pouring into the mountains in search of gold and silver. Word of the area's scenic beauty attracted summer tourists, who lodged in the village's grand log hotels.

Boardwalks stretch the length of Grand Avenue. Buildings with split lodgepole pine facades hold shops, saloons and cafes. Summer nights, the Rocky Mountain Repertory Theatre performs revues and musicals in the community house on Public Square. From the porch at Grand Lake Lodge, a national historic landmark built in 1920, visitors enjoy captivating views of the lakes and surrounding mountains.

Photographs, left to right:
1. Bull elk
2. Summer in Endovalley
3. Wildflowers thrive along a mountain stream.
4. Near the headwaters of the Colorado River

Peak to Peak

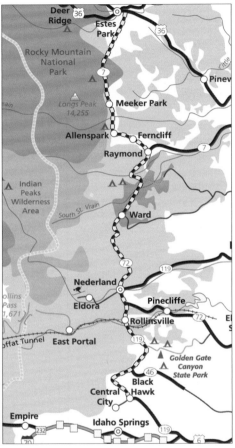

Map of Peak to Peak Byway

Trip Planner: Peak to Peak

Route: Follows Colorado 72 and Colorado 7 between Black Hawk/Central City and Estes Park.

Total length: 55 miles.

Driving time: One and one-half hours, excluding stops.

Outstanding features: Indian Peaks, Mount Meeker, Longs Peak.

Vehicle restrictions: None.

Accessibility: Year-round.

Key events: Madam Lou Bunch Day, Central City, third Saturday of June; Scottish-Irish Highland Festival, Estes Park, weekend after Labor Day.

Contact: Boulder Convention & Visitors Bureau, 303-442-2911, www.bouldercoloradousa.com. Central City Public Information, 800-542-2999, www.centralcityco.org; Estes Park Chamber Resort Association, 970-586-4431, 800-443-7837, www.estesparkresort.com.

Gulch and Estes Park, gateway to Rocky Mountain National Park. Throughout the journey, it captures awe-inspiring views of rugged mountaintops scraping the sky.

The route starts at an elevation above 8,000 feet in the historic mining district occupied by Black Hawk and Central City, once known as

For nearly a century, travelers have cruised along the Peak to Peak Highway to admire the breathtaking scenery of forested slopes, snow-dusted mountains and sweeping vistas. In 1918, the state named the route its first scenic byway. When the Colorado Scenic and Historic Byways program was created in 1989, it was selected as one of the five initial designated routes.

The Peak to Peak Highway parallels the Continental Divide between Black Hawk in Gregory

"the richest square mile on earth." Today, limited-stake gambling casinos and the Central City Opera's summer season lure visitors to the quaint towns. As the road heads up North Clear Creek Canyon, the remains of Golden Gilpin Gold Mill attest to the area's mining heritage.

All along the way, the byway traverses state and national public lands, each offering recreational activities in pristine settings. First comes Arapaho National Forest, then the entrance to Golden Gate Canyon State Park.

The majestic range in Indian Peaks Wilderness Area fills the horizon as the road winds upward. Lush ponderosa pine forests cover the slopes. In autumn, stands of aspen streak the mountainsides with broad swaths of gold. In winter, snow-capped South Arapaho, North Arapaho, Kiowa and Navajo peaks shimmer under the sun like diamonds.

The route enters Rollinsville, which once served as a major railroad hub. Before the Moffat Tunnel was bored, westbound trains chugged over treacherous Rollins Pass. To complete the 23-mile trip, locomotive firemen had to shovel 15 tons of coal into the engine. Today, on winter weekends, the Ski Train whistles through Rollinsville, transporting snow riders to Winter Park Resort.

Photographs, left to right:
1. St. Malo Chapel
2. Mount Meeker
3. Indian Peaks Wilderness Area

After entering Roosevelt National Forest, the byway reaches its halfway point at Nederland. The mountain town has evolved from a mining center to a counterculture haven to an alpine suburb of Boulder. Ore booms in the late 1800s brought so many people to the town that hoteliers rented beds in eight-hour shifts, and restaurants allowed diners only 20 minutes to eat a meal. Today, travelers stop here to explore its arts and crafts galleries, rock shop, museum and riverside trail. A number of eateries, including a Nepalese restaurant, offer a variety of lunch options. In the winter, skiers glide down the slopes of nearby Eldora Mountain Resort.

The road continues winding upward to Ward, where the elevation exceeds 9,600 feet. Mounds of talus ring the former mining camp. In the 1890s, Switzerland Trail of America Railroad operated a daily excursion train to Ward. Passengers thrilled in scaling the mountain to scenic vistas and fresh alpine air. Today, a well-preserved schoolhouse and church remind visitors of the quiet community's golden days.

The highway then descends into Peaceful Valley, a former noontime stop on the Ward-Estes stage run, and enters Middle St. Vrain canyon. When it turns onto Colorado 7, a massive mountain — Mount Meeker — appears on the horizon. The peak was named after Nathan Meeker, founder of the Union Colony at Greeley. Town names such as Ferncliff and Allenspark reveal either the sites' natural features or first homesteaders. Built atop a huge granite rock, St. Malo Chapel graces the roadside.

As it winds down into Tahosa Valley, the byway passes a historic marker honoring Enos Mills. The naturalist's tireless campaign led to creation of Rocky Mountain National Park in 1915. In the distance, a single-room log cabin in which he wrote many of his stories about wildlife and nature stands on land he homesteaded. Across the road is Longs Peak Inn, which Mills owned and operated in the early 1900s. He interpreted nature for his guests and led hundreds of climbs up 14,255-foot Longs Peak.

Farther down the road, the Twin Sisters rise on the east. Six miles before reaching Estes Park, Lily Lake Visitor Center orients travelers to Rocky Mountain National Park. Exhibits give half-day, full-day and multiple-day recommendations for a variety of activities, including birdwatching, wildflower viewing and photography. From this angle, Longs Peak is distinguished by its beaver shape. Across from the center, a groomed gravel path circles Lily Lake. Anglers enjoy catch-and-release fly fishing.

Estes Park, the eastern gateway to Colorado's first national park, lies nestled below in a broad mountain valley. The descent curves through cut rock to the resort town. Elk graze in roadside meadows. In the distance, Mummy Range pinpoints the location of the national park, promising additional wonders for travelers who continue exploring.

Mountaintop Arias

When the 550-seat Central City Opera House opened its doors in 1878, it epitomized the wealth generated by the region's lucrative gold mines. Granite quarried locally formed its elegant structure. A chandelier fashioned with 100 kerosene lamps glowed inside the theater. Elaborate trompe l'oeil murals by San Francisco artist John Massman graced the walls. Misfortune befell the opera house when gold mining waned, forcing its closure in 1927. After intensive fund-raising efforts, it reopened five years later with a festive production of "Camille," starring legendary Lillian Gish. The Central City Opera House Association continues to attract quality operatic and theatrical productions to its stage. Each summer, a blast of miner's dynamite and ringing of the opera bell herald the beginning of the season. "The Ballad of Baby

Doe," which premiered in 1956, has become Central City Opera's signature piece. Opera and stage stars who have performed here have included Beverly Sills, Jerome Hines, Helen Hayes, Mae West, Samuel Ramey and Catherine Malfitano.

Wilderness Act of 1964

Along the Front Range and throughout Colorado, vast wilderness areas beautify the landscape. Within their boundaries, the Wilderness Act of 1964 prohibits logging, mining and road building, permanent structures and commercial enterprises, and all mechanized vehicles. It does permit livestock grazing, hunting and fishing. Through this landmark legislation, the U.S. Congress expressed its desire to keep selected federal lands undisturbed by human settlement and mechanization by defining wilderness as "an area untrammeled by man, where man himself is a visitor who does not remain."

Estes Park

The eastern gateway to Rocky Mountain National Park percolates with activity. True to its western heritage, the area hosts horse shows and rodeos. Cow pokes find a number of places to horseback ride. While serious anglers gravitate to Lake Estes or mountain streams, novices hook their first "big ones" at stocked trout ponds. Trails perfect for hiking, cross-country skiing and snowshoeing lace the surrounding forests. Elk and deer often treat visitors to wildlife viewing right in town.

Cultural offerings range from concerts by chamber orchestras and jazz ensembles to contemporary theater. In addition, art galleries showcase works by more than 200 artists. Each September, the Fine Arts Guild sponsors the Juried Fine Arts and Crafts Festival. Several museums chronicle Estes Park's early years and leaders. The MacGregor Ranch Museum, for example, shows how one family's homestead evolved over three generations.

Shoppers encounter a bonanza of stores selling everything from handcrafted jewelry and collectors' items to that "must have" souvenir. Some 60 restaurants and eateries satisfy a breadth of tastes and budgets. Lodging options also abound. Visitors can choose from rustic cabins to cozy bed-and-breakfasts, riverside lodges and the Stanley Hotel's vintage elegance.

Photographs, left to right:
1. Lake Isabel nestles among the Indian Peaks.
2. Homestead cabin of naturalist Enos Mills
3. Man in full regalia at Scottish-Irish Highland Festival
4. The historic Stanley Hotel opened in 1909.

Mount Evans

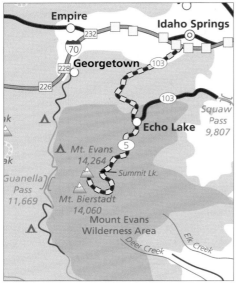

Map of Mount Evans Byway

Trip Planner: Mount Evans

Route: Follows Colorado 103 from Idaho Springs to Echo Lake, then climbs Colorado 5 to the summit.

Total length: 28 miles one way.

Driving time: Two hours round trip, excluding stops.

Outstanding features: Mount Evans summit, mountain goats and Rocky Mountain bighorn sheep, bristlecone pine forest, wildflowers, extraordinary panoramas.

Vehicle restrictions: None.

Accessibility: Segment from Idaho Springs to Echo Lake (Colorado 103) is open to vehicles year-round. The segment from the fee station at Echo Lake to the summit (Colorado 5) typically is open from Memorial Day to Labor Day, longer if weather permits.

Special considerations: Use low gear to minimize wear on brakes. Sudden weather changes are common.

Key events: Gold Rush Days, Idaho Springs, third weekend of August.

Fee: A fee applies to the segment from Echo Lake to the summit.

Contact: USFS-Clear Creek Ranger District, 303-567-2901, Idaho Springs Visitor Center, 800-882-5278, www.clearcreekcounty.org.

Chilling winds whistle as byway travelers leave the comfort of their cars to scale the final 130 vertical feet to the summit of Mount Evans. The trail zigs and zags upward. Although the distance is only a quarter mile, muscles burn and lungs crave oxygen. Within minutes, though, climbers stand on top of the world.

The thrilling quest to the top climaxes a byway journey filled with wondrous natural sights. Among them are ancient trees that have lived longer than Methuselah, mountain goats balancing atop craggy rocks and permafrost rarely found outside of the Arctic tundra.

Starting in Idaho Springs, the road winds through Arapaho National Forest on Colorado 103 to Echo Lake. Ore tailings attest to the region's mining era. As the altitude increases, ponderosa pine and blue spruce forests give way to towering lodgepole pines. Stands of aspen carpet entire slopes, promising gold-bullion radiance in the autumn.

Mount Evans' massif rises into full view. At Ponder Point, travelers can pull off to admire its raw grandeur.

Midway up the route, the elevation reaches two miles above sea level. Anglers cast their lines into shimmering Echo Lake. Its lakeside picnic ground offers a restful spot to have lunch before continuing the ascent.

At the end of the lake, the byway turns onto Colorado 5 and enters the Mount Evans Wilderness Area. Sub-alpine fir and Engelmann spruce trees anchor their roots in thin topsoil, bending and dwarfing into krummholz (crooked trees) as the elevation nears timberline.

One of Colorado's few stands of bristlecone pines highlights Mount Goliath Natural Area. Despite dry, brutal winds, little precipitation and extreme temperatures, many of these extraordinary trees are more than 1,500 years old. On Bristlecone Pine Loop, visitors can stroll among these twisted and gnarled survivors.

Photographs, left to right:
1. Mountain goats scale craggy rocks.
2. Visitors climb to the summit of Mount Evans.
3. The byway winds through tundra.

Several times a day, forest rangers lead nature walks on M. Walter Pesman Trail from Lower Goliath Trailhead. On the moderately difficult 1.5-mile route, visitors learn hints for identifying wildflowers. The Old Man of the Mountain, for example, wears a "hairy coat" on its stem. Bistort smells like dirty socks. And whereas queen's crown is cone-shaped, king's crown is flat-topped.

Alpine Loop, located at Upper Goliath Trailhead, offers a shorter wildflower hike. Rangers keep a weekly list of blossoming flowers to assist those exploring on their own.

As the byway climbs above timberline, a thin turf of cushion plants, grasses and sedges carpets the landscape. At 12,800 feet, partially frozen Summit Lake glistens. Permafrost, or permanently frozen ground, distinguishes this alpine area. Tiny tundra flowers hug the soil. A short hike beyond the lake opens onto a striking view of the glaciated valley of Chicago Creek.

Wildlife, including bighorn sheep, marmots and ptarmigans, thrive here. On summer weekends, Colorado Division of Wildlife volunteers help visitors identify animals' distinguishing characteristics with displays of pelts and horns, and by viewing them with spotting scopes. Mountain goats, for example, have long, white hair and black, spiked horns. In comparison, Rocky Mountain bighorn sheep sport buff-brown coats, and the rams have massive, curled horns.

The road's final ascent winds through

expansive fields strewn with boulders and dappled with small snowfields. The dark, jagged profile of Sawtooth Range rises to the west. In a deep valley, an alpine lake mirrors the sky.

A mere 130 feet below Mount Evans' summit, the road ends in a parking lot. Travelers pull on fleeces and jackets to protect against the wind and a temperature at least 30 degrees cooler than Denver. Whether clouds envelope the massif with mist or the sun shines brightly, being atop this mountain inspires awe.

While visitors explore, white-haired mountain goats may be standing just a few feet away, licking gneiss and granite rocks for their minerals. Or they may bound from boulder to boulder.

On a clear day, spectacular vistas display Colorado's landmarks like a topographical map. To the north, Longs Peak and other high summits of Rocky Mountain National Park tower. To the east, the prairie rolls to the horizon. From southeast to southwest, the vista crescendos from Pikes Peak to the Sangre de Cristos to South Park to the Collegiate Range. To the immediate west, visitors can look down upon the dome of Mount Bierstadt.

Travelers can take in these sights from various points in the parking lot, but the best view requires hiking the strenuous quarter-mile trail to the 14,264-foot summit. The reward for reaching "the top of the world" more than makes up for the effort—a glorious 360-degree panorama of Colorado's mountains and plains.

Bristlecone Pines

Twisted and contorted, these tenacious trees survive the incredibly harsh conditions of altitudes ranging from 8,000 to 12,000 feet. Unrelenting winds, scant moisture, intense sunlight, sub-zero temperatures, a short growing season, and dry, shallow soil threaten their survival. Yet many are more than 1,500 years old. Size can be deceptive. A six-foot bristlecone pine may have taken seed about the time that Christopher Columbus landed in the Western Hemisphere. It can take a century for a trunk to grow an inch in diameter. Punishing winds have sculpted many of these pines into flag trees, with barren windward sides and branches stretching leeward. The end of each cone scale sports a

bristle-like point, thus the name bristlecone pine. Byway travelers can walk among these ancient survivors in the Mount Goliath Natural Area.

Colorado's State Animal

Rocky Mountain bighorn sheep bound up the cliff faces and leap over the yawning crevasses of Colorado's rugged ranges. Massive curled horns crown the rams. Making up 10 percent of a male's body weight, they weigh up to 25 pounds and may grow 50 inches long. As part of the mating ritual, males butt their horns to assert dominance and increase their chances of breeding. They charge each other at speeds up to 40 mph. The rut begins in late fall. Lambs are usually born in May or June. Ewes also have horns. Theirs, however, are straight, 8- to 10-inch spikes. Both sexes have rich, tan, double-layered coats. Shed each spring, they grow anew by late summer. The animals' digestive systems make it possible to graze large amounts of forage rapidly and then retreat to ledges where they can chew and digest it safe from predators.

Photographs, left to right:
1. Mountain goats above Abyss Lake
2. Many bristlecone pines are more than 1,500 years old.
3. Wildflowers ring Summit Lake.
4. Rocky Mountain bighorn sheep

Keen eyesight, sharp hearing and a highly developed sense of smell alert them to danger. Their average life span is eight years. Although the number of Rocky Mountain bighorn sheep within the state is far fewer than the thousands that grazed here in the 1800s, Colorado reportedly is home to the largest population of the species anywhere. Travelers can spot Colorado's state animal on rugged slopes and mountain meadows at elevations above 8,000 feet. Prime viewing locations are Interstate 70 at Georgetown, Poudre Canyon near Fort Collins, Sheep Lakes in Rocky Mountain National Park and Mount Evans.

Idaho Springs

The slope facing Idaho Springs bears the town's most noticeable landmark, Bridal Veil Falls cascading onto an 1890s waterwheel. Ironically, the miner who built it attributed his robust health to never shaving or bathing. In winter, the water freezes into a dramatic ice sculpture, and during NFL playoffs locals often dye it Denver Broncos orange.

Area mines still extract precious ore. Visitors can learn about mining history during tours of the Argo Gold Mine-Mill-Museum, Edgar Experimental Mine and Phoenix Mine. The Heritage Museum and Visitors Center chronicles Idaho Springs' early years with exhibits ranging from Native American artifacts to vintage fire department equipment.

For relaxation, bathers soak in Indian Hot Springs' natural mineral waters. On Miner Street, restored Victorian buildings house restaurants and a variety of shops to explore.

Guanella Pass

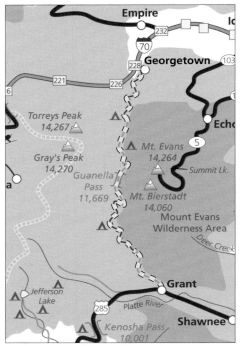

Map of Guanella Pass Byway

Vast tundra carpeted with vibrant wildflowers in the summer and windswept snow in the winter greets travelers at the summit of Guanella Pass byway. Rugged ridges scrape the sky. At lower elevations, mountain creeks transform into shimmering lakes and waterfalls.

The 22-mile route runs between Georgetown and Grant, mountain communities that date from the 19th-century mining boom. Area silver mines buffed Georgetown into an affluent commercial and residential center. On the south side of Guanella Pass, Grant emerged as a small supply and lumber town.

Starting in Georgetown at an elevation of 8,500 feet, the road climbs up a series of switchbacks through thick stands of blue spruce, Douglas fir, and lodgepole pine laced with aspen. Pullouts capture glorious views of the Victorian village cradled in the valley below. Old mine

tailings blotch slopes with golden-brown mounds. In autumn, aspens streak the forests with honey-colored hues.

The byway follows South Clear Creek past the remains of Silverdale, a former mining camp. Throughout the moist riparian ecosystem, abundant shrubs and grasses thrive.

A series of lakes sculpted by ancient glaciers mirror the sky. Clear Lake offers a prime spot to picnic and fish. The paved road becomes dirt at the Cabin Creek Hydroelectric Generation Plant, which from this remote location

monitors and maintains the Georgetown hydro-electric facility.

As the byway winds upward, the creek meanders through willow thickets and tumbles over tiers of beaver dams. Wilson's warblers, white-crowned sparrows and other songbirds chirp and trill. In summer, blue columbines dapple dark forest floors. Mule deer prong through the trees.

Higher elevations reveal the effects of fierce winds and extreme weather. Trees grow branches only on the leeward side and bend into dense low growth called krummholz (crooked trees).

Cirques, craggy ridges and the absence of trees herald the summit. Cresting at 11,669 feet, the pass is named for Paul Byron Guanella, a devoted county commissioner and highway supervisor instrumental in the construction of this road.

Dramatic mountains encircle the broad, gently rolling tundra. Mount Bierstadt towers in the foreground. The fourteener bears the name of the celebrated 19th–century Western landscape artist, Albert Bierstadt. Sawtooth Ridge connects it with Mount Evans to the east. Grays and Torreys peaks bejewel the western horizon.

Trails lead from the pass's parking lot over boggy terrain to Mount Bierstadt, Mount Rosalie (named after the artist's wife) and the Mount Evans Wilderness Area. During wildflower season, yellow cinquefoil, Indian paintbrush, chiming blue bells and white tuft speckle the alpine meadow. In winter, deep, windswept snow caps the tundra, creating a crystalline landscape for snowshoers and cross-country skiers to explore.

A flock of ptarmigans lives on the pass year round. Camouflaged by pure white feathers in winter and mottled brown ones in summer, they are difficult to spot. Snowshoe hares, marmots and pikas also reside in this habitat.

As it descends from the summit, the steep, narrow byway switchbacks past a large natural body of water, Duck Lake, and defunct Geneva Basin ski area. A turnoff on a four-wheel-drive road leads to the ghost town of Geneva City. Below timberline, forests of Engelmann spruce and subalpine fir cover the slopes.

Paralleling Duck Creek, the road reaches the edge of Geneva Park. Bighorn sheep frequent the area. In summer, the large mountain meadow turns blue with columbines. The

Photographs, left to right:
1. Towering peaks rim the tundra at Guanella Pass.
2. South Clear Creek sustains wetlands.
3. Water cascades down Falls Hill.

gravel road then descends through Geneva Creek Canyon. Water cascades 300 feet down Falls Hill, filling the air with its serenade. Round boulders, which glaciers polished eons ago, stud the fields.

Thick stands of blue spruce, pine and aspen border the route as it winds alongside Geneva Creek. The sound of rushing water mixed with the forest's sweet perfume creates inviting settings for the roadside picnic areas.

At the tiny settlement of Grant, the road reaches its southern end. From here, travelers can return to their homes via U.S. 285 or retrace the byway to explore Georgetown.

Once known as the Silver Queen of the Rockies, this charming historic community features fun shops, tasty food, entertaining museums, the famous Georgetown Loop Railroad and Georgetown Lake's wildlife viewing area. When serendipity prevails, travelers spot Rocky Mountain bighorn sheep scaling rugged slopes.

Powerful Water

History and function converge at the Georgetown Energy Museum, a fully functioning and operating hydroelectric generating plant. In the early 1900s, the facility began supplying power to Georgetown, Silver Plume, Idaho Springs, Black Hawk, Central City and mines in the area. Inside the plant, visitors watch its two water wheel generator sets operate. Water from Georgetown Reservoir, located about a mile up the Guanella Pass byway, drives the wheels. The 700-foot vertical fall from the reservoir to the plant produces 275 pounds per square inch of water pressure at the water wheels. The Cabin Creek Hydroelectric Plant maintains and monitors the facility remotely from its site five miles up the byway. Museum tours highlight the history of hydroelectric power. Exhibits include photographs and early appliances.

[600 Griffith St., Georgetown; 303-569-3557; free; open June through first week of October and Christmas Market weekends.]

How and When Aspen Change Color

Shimmering in the sunlight like gold coins, aspen leaves herald autumn with their stunning brilliant yellow hue, often tinged red or orange. A complex natural process underlies this color change. Throughout the spring and summer, leaf cells containing the green pigment chlorophyll conduct photosynthesis, which transforms sunshine into food necessary for the trees' growth. The green color predominates, masking yellow and orange pigments also

present in the leaves. When the length of daylight shortens and temperatures begin to fall, a cyst forms at the base of the leafstalk. This prevents the intake of water and other nutrients required to make chlorophyll, causing it to break down. As a result, the leaves' green color gradually disappears and the hidden yellow, orange and red pigments become visible. By mid-September, aspens begin to paint mountain slopes with golden splendor.

Georgetown

More than 200 charming historic buildings and homes beautify Georgetown. Its quaint neighborhoods, entertaining attractions and diverse stores invite travelers to stop and explore.

At the Hamill House Museum, visitors learn about the lifestyle of a silver magnate. The Hotel de Paris shows the posh environs enjoyed in the 1870s by traveling businessmen. Amenities included steam heat, running water and elegant dining. Railroad enthusiasts gravitate to the Georgetown Loop Railroad to experience its extraordinary engineering feat – 4 1/2 miles of narrow-gauge tracks in a distance of two miles. The ride along aspen-laced slopes also includes a visit to the historic Lebanon Mine and Mill Complex.

Along the Sixth Street business district, visitors enjoy antique shops, boutiques, art galleries and a variety of restaurants. In addition, annual events celebrate Georgetown's heritage. During the old-fashioned Fourth of July festival, teams of firemen compete to unwind and connect the hoses of vintage firehose carts in record time. Every December, the Christmas Market features musical performances, tours of landmark homes and outdoor stalls selling quilts, baked goods and ornaments. The Santa Lucia Children's Processional spreads the happiness of the season as the youngsters carol in the streets.

Photographs, left to right:
1. Historic buildings beautify Georgetown.
2. Locomotive chugs atop the Georgetown Loop.
3. Geneva Creek
4. Horseback riders enjoy mountain vistas.

Lariat Loop

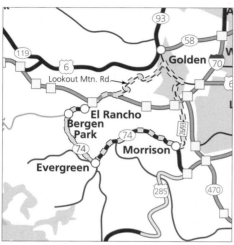

Map of Lariat Loop Byway

Trip Planner: Lariat Loop

Route: The byway connects Golden, Lookout Mountain, Evergreen and Morrison. It heads west from Golden up Lookout Mountain Road, follows Interstate 70 from Genesee Park Exit 254 to Hwy. 74 Exit 252, follows Hwy. 74 south to Evergreen and east to Morrison, and turns north on Hwy. 26/93 and Heritage Road to Golden.

Total length: 40 miles.

Driving time: One hour, excluding stops.

Outstanding features: Lookout Mountain, Genesee Mountain, buffalo herd, Bear Creek Canyon, Red Rocks Park & Amphitheatre, Dinosaur Ridge.

Vehicle restrictions: None.

Accessibility: Year-round.

Key events: Buffalo Bill Days, Golden, fourth weekend of July; Skate the Lake, Evergreen, New Year's Eve.

Contact: Lariat Loop Heritage Alliance, 303-697-3466 ext. 11, info@lariatloop.org, www.lariatloop.org. Greater Golden Chamber of Commerce, 303-279-3113, 800-590-3113, www.goldencochamber.org; Evergreen Area Chamber of Commerce, 303-674-3412, www.evergreenchamber.org; Morrison Town Office, 303-697-8749, www.town.morrison.co.us

Colorado's newest scenic and historic by-way, the Lariat Loop, winds among the foothills rising to the west of Denver. Designated in 2002, it is unique in its proximity to a major metropolitan area.

The 40-mile route highlights stunning geological formations, expansive mountain parks and rich history. From dinosaur tracks and grazing buffalo to tumbling streams and soaring peaks, a smorgasbord of fascinating sights greets travelers.

The lasso connects Golden, Lookout Mountain, Evergreen and Morrison. The gateway to historic Lariat Trail, which climbs the face of Lookout Mountain, offers an impressive starting point for exploring the byway. Towering sandstone pillars dating to 1913 still mark the entrance. The route follows 19th Street west from its juncture with U.S. 6 in Golden to the gateway, where it begins the climb.

While hikers and mountain bikers scale the steep slope, bicyclists and cars negotiate the road's tight curves. The town of Golden nestles in the valley below. Overhead, paragliders sail on wind currents.

On the top of Lookout Mountain, the Buffalo Bill Museum & Grave relates the legendary life of William F. Cody. Exhibits portray his extraordinary experiences as a Pony Express rider, scout and Wild West showman. From the grave site, a sweeping panorama of metropolitan Denver unfolds.

Nearby, the Lookout Mountain Nature Center and Preserve acquaints visitors with migratory birds and the ponderosa pine forest. Mule deer, Abert squirrels and other wildlife often appear along the trails winding through the Jefferson County Open Space park. The former

summer home and hunting lodge of Denver entrepreneur and philanthropist, Charles Boettcher, stands next door. Featuring Craftsman-style details, the Boettcher Mansion currently serves as a special events site.

From there, Lookout Mountain Road turns west, paralleling Interstate 70 to the Genesee Park exit. Sublime views of the Continental Divide fill the western horizon. A herd of American bison, owned by the city and county of Denver, grazes in Genesee Mountain Park, often within photographing distance. The park also contains Chief Hosa Lodge and Campground. Built of hand-cut Colorado granite, the historic structure holds receptions and other gatherings.

The byway then merges onto I-70 west as far as Exit 252 and follows Hwy. 74 south to Evergreen. Along the way it skirts several Denver Mountain Parks and Jefferson County Open Spaces, ideal for hiking and picnicking. Evergreen Lake glistens in its mountain setting. During the winter, skaters lace up at the Lake House and glide the ice. In Evergreen, shops and restaurants hug the main street. Two historic sites, the Humphrey Memorial Park & Museum and the Hiwan Homestead Museum, depict the lifestyles of early residents. The latter also displays an impressive array of Native American handicrafts.

Following Bear Creek northeast, the route winds through narrow Bear Creek Canyon. Jefferson County and Denver parks border much of this stretch, preserving the area for wildlife viewing, hiking and other mountain recreation. Along the way, the road passes through the communities of Kittredge and Idledale. Bear Creek Canyon Park, undeveloped open space acquired by Denver in 1928, extends four miles from Idledale to Morrison and offers fishing access.

In the quaint town of Morrison, travelers can browse through antique and curio shops, visit the Heritage Museum or grab a bite to eat in one of the family restaurants. Scores of the town's businesses, churches and homes occupy buildings that date from the late 19th century. In the Morrison Natural History Museum, visitors learn about the various dinosaurs discovered in Colorado and how to extract fossils from rock.

The byway turns north on Colorado 26/93 to Red Rocks Park & Amphitheatre, another Denver Mountain Park. Towering sandstone formations named Creation, Ship Rock and Stage Rock form the world-renowned outdoor concert venue. Celebrities from the Beatles to the Blues Travelers have performed here. Both the amphitheater's infrastructure and the Trading Post were built in the 1930s by the Civilian Conservation Corps. These sites offer spectacular vistas of the park's geological wonders.

Across the way, dinosaur tracks etch Dinosaur Ridge. Interpretive stops in the National Natural Landmark also point out dinosaur bones, trace fossils and other ancient features.

As the route continues north, the Mother Cabrini Shrine comes into view. The serene hilltop site serves as a place of pilgrimage and prayer.

The Lariat Loop reaches its end in Golden. Here, travelers can tour museums, browse art galleries, shop and dine. The former territorial capital of Colorado also brims with sites that chronicle its rich history.

Clear Creek tumbles through downtown.

Driving a few miles up Clear Creek Canyon offers one last encounter with the area's natural beauty – and the possibility of spotting an eagle.

Denver Mountain Parks

A buffalo herd, historic stagecoach toll station and Braille trail are some of the unique features found in the Denver Mountain Park system. The city and county of Denver established its first and largest mountain park – Genesee Park — in 1912. Today, it owns and operates 14,000 acres of Colorado mountain and foothills property, divided into 46 parcels.

More than a dozen of these parks enhance the scenery enjoyed along the Lariat Loop byway. Two popular trails course through Genesee Park. Braille Trail leads blind hikers with interpretive signs in Braille and waist-high guide wire. Beaver Brook Trail challenges hikers with a strenuous backcountry trek. Visitors can picnic under a beautiful stone shelter built in 1939 by the Civilian Conservation Corps. The city's buffalo herd grazes on park slopes bordering Interstate 70.

In Lookout Mountain Park, travelers can experience western lore and artifacts at the Buffalo Bill Museum & Grave and Pahaska Tepee Gift Shop. In comparison, Bear Creek Canyon Park is an undeveloped open space that runs four miles along Bear Creek and offers fishing access. Extraordinary geological features distinguish Red Rocks Park, located 15 miles west of downtown Denver. Sandstone formations create a natural amphitheatre in which concerts, opera and stage productions are performed. Visitors can further explore the park's natural beauty on extensive hiking trails.

To make these mountain parklands accessible to Denver residents in the early 20th century, the city developed a premier road system. Two of its scenic mountain drives, the Lariat Trail and Bear Creek Canyon, form major

Photographs, left to right:
1. Colorado Railroad Museum displays locomotives.
2. Cowboy sculpture at Hiwan Homestead Museum
3. Legendary Buffalo Bill is buried on Lookout Mountain.
4. Costumed interpreter cooks at Clear Creek History Park.

segments of the Lariat Loop Scenic and Historic Byway.

Dinosaur Ridge

Hundreds of dinosaur footprints and bones embed the slopes of Dinosaur Ridge, located only 15 miles west of downtown Denver. The National Natural Landmark showcases ancient fossils, dinosaur tracks and striking geological features at 16 interpretive stops. Evidence of the site's paleontological treasures was first discovered in 1877 when a teacher, Arthur Lakes, happened upon some large dinosaur bones along the ridge's west slope. Subsequent excavations unearthed the first stegosaurus armatus fossil. Fossilized bones of apatosaurus, diplodocus and other dinosaurs were also found. Many bones can still be seen.

Another discovery occurred 50 years later (1937) when construction of Alameda Parkway exposed dinosaur tracks on the ridge's east slope. Today more than 300 footprints left by two types of dinosaurs are viewable. Iguanodons, which were herbivores, pressed their broad, three-toed hind feet into the earth. Their front feet formed smaller, crescent-shaped tracks. The other dinosaurs were ostrich-size, carnivorous ornithomimous. Walking only on their hind feet, they left three-pronged footprints that resemble large bird tracks.

The mile-long stretch of Alameda Parkway that traverses Dinosaur Ridge provides access to the landmark's sites. As the road climbs up the east side of the ridge, sweeping views of metropolitan Denver and the plains stretch to the horizon. Signs point out plant and invertebrate fossils, evidence of ancient beaches and remnants of volcanic eruptions. On the descent, the west slope treats travelers to a vista of Red Rocks Park's stunning sandstone formations.

[Friends of Dinosaur Ridge 303-697-3466, www.dinoridge.org, 16831 W. Alameda Parkway, Morrison; free; open year-round.]

Golden

"Howdy Folks! Welcome to Golden" proclaims the sign that arcs over the town's main street. Nestled along Clear Creek between the Front Range foothills and the Table Mountains, the community offers an array of entertaining activities.

Displaying vintage barber shop signs and other quaint items, Foss General Store sells almost anything imaginable. Foothills Art Center showcases outstanding exhibitions of watercolor paintings, ceramics and other media. The Rocky Mountain Quilt Museum preserves nearly 200 heritage quilts.

Many sites celebrate Golden's early days as Colorado's territorial capital and a bustling railroad hub that supplied the Rockies' booming gold mines. Among them are Clear Creek History Park, a living history museum, and Astor House Museum, which served as a residence for territorial legislators. The Colorado Railroad Museum exhibits vintage locomotives and railcars that once scaled mountain railways. The Colorado School of Mines Geology Museum chronicles the region's mining history and showcases thousands of minerals, fossils, rocks and gemstones.

Sightseers can also take a look at the town's current economic activity. Dating from 1873, Coors Brewing Company offers free tours. In the National Renewable Energy Laboratory visitor center, exhibits describe wind, solar, biomass and other leading-edge renewable energy and energy efficient technologies.

In the summertime, kayakers streak through the slalom course set up in Clear Creek between 10th and 11th Avenues. On the edge of Golden, hiking and mountain biking trails thread up Lookout Mountain, which bears the letter 'M" for the town's renowned Colorado School of Mines. The view from the summit captures a sweeping vista of metropolitan Denver and the high plains.

Photograph this page:
Golden greets visitors.
Opposite page: Mount Elbert (14,433') is
Colorado's highest peak.

Top of the Rockies

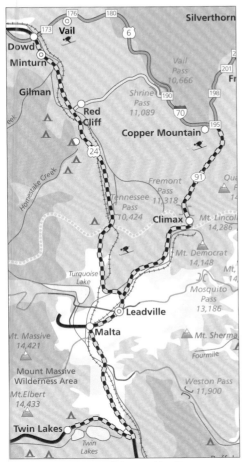

Map of Top of the Rockies Byway

Trip Planner: Top of the Rockies

Route: Follows Colorado 91 from Copper Mountain to Leadville, then north on U.S. 24 to Minturn. A spur follows U.S. 24 south from Leadville to Colorado 82, then west to Twin Lakes.
Total length: 82 miles.
Driving time: Two hours, excluding stops.
Outstanding features: Tennessee and Fremont passes, Arkansas Headwaters State Recreation Area, Mount Elbert and Mount Massive, Camp Hale.
Vehicle restrictions: None.
Accessibility: Year-round.
Key events: Leadville Boom Days, Leadville, first weekend of August.
Contact: Leadville and Lake County Chamber of Commerce, 800-933-3901, 719-486-3900, www.leadvilleusa.com. Copper Mountain Resort Chamber, 970-968-6477, www.coppercolorado.com.

As it winds through mountain terrain at elevations typically exceeding 9,000 feet, the Top of the Rockies byway reveals sublime alpine vistas. It crosses the Continental Divide twice, parallels the highest range in the U.S. Rockies, and passes through quaint historic towns.

Starting at Copper Mountain Resort, the 75-mile highway heads south through Tenmile Creek Valley. A scenic overlook captures Mount of the Holy Cross, whose cross-shaped snowfield can usually be seen from mid-June through mid-July. Also viewable are Sheep Mountain, Notch Mountain and Whitney Peak.

When the route reaches the 11,318-foot summit of Fremont Pass, it crosses the Continental Divide. Water falling east of the divide flows to the Atlantic Ocean; water falling west of it flows to the Pacific Ocean.

Scraped, stripped and cratered slopes pocked with tailing ponds mark the site of the Climax Molybdenum Mine. Thirty miles of underground tunnels and railroad tracks

honeycomb Bartlet Mountain. Directly across from the mine entrance, a pullout contains weather-beaten interpretive panels that describe the history and uses of the ore, as well as mining and milling processes.

From there, the road enters a broad meadow filled with willow bushes. On clear days, Mount Elbert, Colorado's tallest mountain, comes into full view.

The historic mining town of Leadville sits at the lofty elevation of 10,152 feet. The area's rich lodes turned legendary Horace Tabor and other investors into instant millionaires. The Silver Dollar Saloon, Delaware Hotel and other distinctive buildings dating from Leadville's halcyon years line Harrison Avenue. The "Route of the Silver Kings," a self-guided automobile tour, features mine shafts and other remnants of the Leadville mining district.

South of town, a red, one-room schoolhouse brightens the former smelting town of Malta. County Road 300 leads west to the Leadville National Fish Hatchery, built in 1890. In addition to fish raceways and a historic visitor center, the site has several nature trails to explore.

As the byway travels south on U.S. 24, it parallels the jagged Sawatch Range, the highest of the U.S. Rockies. Colorado's two tallest peaks, Mount Elbert (14,433 feet) and Mount Massive (14,421 feet) soar skyward.

The wide Arkansas River Valley lies between the highway and the range. From its headwaters on the south side of Fremont Pass, the Arkansas River begins its 1,300-mile journey to the Mississippi River. The Arkansas Headwaters Recreation Area straddles the river, offering numerous outdoor activities, from trout fishing to cross-country skiing. Emphasizing the importance of this route as a communications link, a former wagon toll road, stagecoach route and railroad run alongside the byway.

Piles of rock resulting from 19th-century placer and hydraulic mining herald the turn onto Colorado 82. Rolling hills dotted with sagebrush rise on either side of the road. On the horizon, towering peaks frame the shimmering Twin Lakes. Forests laced with aspens climb the slopes to timberline.

In the tiny 1870s village of Twin Lakes, B&Bs offer quiet getaways. Painted bright red, the general store also serves as a post office and gas station. A local park features an assay office, hotel, log cabin and other historic buildings. Nearby, a short forest trail climbs to views of glacially sculpted Twin Peaks, Mount Hope, Quail Mountain and Parry Peak.

The remaining segment of the byway, also known as the 10th Mountain Division Memorial Highway, is accessed by retracing the route to Leadville and continuing north on U.S. 24. The Sawatch Range stretches along a valley covered with cattle ranches.

As the road climbs over 10,424-foot Tennessee Pass, it crosses the Continental Divide

again. A memorial at the top of the pass commemorates the 10th Mountain Division, the first division of the U.S. Army organized and trained to combat as ski and mountain troops. Many of its veterans were the founders and promoters of Colorado's ski areas. A side road leads to Ski Cooper where snowriders can snowboard as well as downhill, cross-country and back-country ski at Chicago Ridge.

Remains of Camp Hale, the 10th Mountain Division training site, etch flat, expansive Pando Valley. Old building foundations can be viewed from an overlook or on a self-guided tour.

In wildflower season, daisies, penstemons and other perky blossoms dapple the roadside. Farther north, a side road leads into a steep canyon to the quaint mining town of Red Cliff. Elegant restored Victorian residences and ramshackle houses stand side by side.

The byway then parallels the Eagle River. Gilman, once a bustling mining and milling center, clings to the side of Battle Mountain. Abandoned in 1984, the houses stand eerily empty.

As the road threads through Eagle River Canyon, it opens to views of meadows and forests. Then it reaches Minturn. The former

railroad town now serves as the gateway to the Holy Cross Wilderness Area.

The byway ends at Dowd Junction where travelers can learn about area wildlife at the Holy Cross Ranger District's information center. They can also spot animals through free distance viewing scopes. Today, North America's largest herd of elk resides in White River National Forest. During the winter, scores of them graze on nearby sun-drenched slopes.

Peak Training

While frigid winds sliced through Camp Hale, soldiers of the 10th Mountain Division honed winter warfare maneuvers. All volunteers, they left jobs ranging from lumberjack and cowboy to college professor. Carrying 80-pound packs and rifles, they learned to ski at night and scale icy cliffs. The post opened in late 1942 in the Pando Valley near Leadville complete with parade grounds, weapons ranges and more than 1,000 structures. During its short existence, Camp Hale forged 15,000 soldiers into the elite outfit whose great World War II offensive in the Apennines led to the unconditional surrender of the German forces in Italy. The division's valor resulted in huge casualties: 992 dead, some 4,000 wounded. Today, a self-guided tour of the camp leads visitors past training sites and the foundations of mule barns, theaters and various other facilities.

Feeding Small Fry

For more than 100 years, the Leadville National Fish Hatchery has supplied Rocky Mountain area streams and lakes with brook, brown,

Photographs, left to right:
1. *Malta's one-room schoolhouse*
2. *Leadville mining ruins*
3. *Climax Molybdenum Mine site*
4. *Shops on Minturn's main street*

cutthroat and rainbow trout. Noting Leadville's cold, clean water supply and nearby sources of native cutthroat trout, the U.S. Congress established a federal hatchery on the east slope of Mount Massive at the lofty elevation of 10,000 feet. In spring 1891, waters in Colorado, Nebraska and South Dakota received the facility's first distribution of trout.

Listed on the National Register of Historic Places, the original, native red sandstone hatchery building graces the grounds. Inside, a visitor center exhibits educational panels that explain the fish farming process from spawning to stocking streams and displays incubators, feeding tanks and other hatchery equipment. Outside, specimens of various trout species swim in a pool. Workers regularly feed fry, or young fish, in outdoor tanks called raceways. A tank of one-year-old trout may contain up to 20,000 fish.

The hatchery tends the fry until they measure about two inches long, then places them in the nearby Evergreen Lakes to continue growing. When the fish have reached the right size, specially equipped tank trucks transport them to select public streams and lakes. Today the hatchery annually produces more than half a million trout that stock Colorado waters.

[Six miles southwest of Leadville on State Highway 300, (719) 486-0189; free; open year-round.]

Leadville

Situated in rarified air at 10,152 feet, Leadville owes its existence to the fortunes of gold, silver, molybdenum and other minerals extracted from the surrounding mountains. The 1880s silver boom created the community of Victorian buildings evident today. Leadville's National Historic Landmark District preserves 70 square blocks of original structures.

Both the walking tour along the main thoroughfare, Harrison Avenue, and the Silver Kings Heritage Driving Tour through the mining district capture the flavor of Leadville's boomtown years. Several attractions also chronicle the mining era. These include the Tabor Opera House, the National Mining Hall of Fame & Museum, Matchless Mine, the Heritage Museum, Healy House and Dexter Cabin.

Excursions on the Leadville, Colorado and Southern Railroad combine both history and scenery. Departing from a historic depot, the train follows the Arkansas River for 11 miles to Fremont Pass.

For outdoor enthusiasts, the Leadville area offers numerous trails for mountain biking, streams for fishing, fourteeners for climbing and rugged mountain roads for four-wheel driving. In winter, snowriders can head to nearby Ski Cooper or venture into the backcountry.

Photographs this page:
1. Camp Hale Site in Pando Valley
2. Leadville's historic main street

Gold Belt Tour

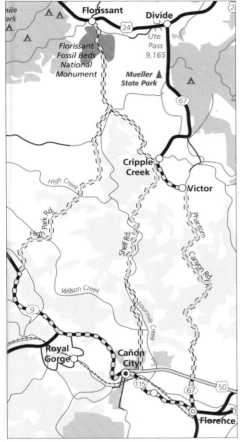

Map of Gold Belt Tour Byway

Route: Follows Teller County Road 1 southbound from Florissant, then splits into three segments. High Park Road heads southwest and then joins Colorado 9 south to U.S. 50, which it follows east to Cañon City. Shelf Road starts at Cripple Creek and heads due south to Cañon City. Phantom Canyon Road starts in Cripple Creek, heads southeast to Victor and then south to Florence. At the byway's southern end, Colorado 115 and U.S. 50 connect the three segments.

Total length: 131 miles.

Driving time: Six hours to drive all segments, excluding stops. Times for the different segments are: 0.5 hour for Teller 1, 1.5 hours for High Park Road, and at least two hours each for Phantom Canyon and Shelf roads.

Outstanding features: The Shelf, sheer canyons, red rock formations, Florissant Fossil Beds National Monument, Pikes Peak, Mount Pisgah.

Vehicle restrictions: A 4-wheel-drive vehicle is recommended on The Shelf and may be necessary when the surface is wet. Do not attempt Phantom Canyon Road or the upper portion of Shelf Road if traveling with a trailer, camper or motor home. Vehicles more than 25 feet long are not permitted on Phantom Canyon Road.

Accessibility: Open year-round.

Special considerations: Avoid Phantom Canyon Road and the upper portion of Shelf Road in wet weather. The latter is narrow with curves and steep drop-offs. Both roads are unpaved. On the one-lane stretch of Shelf Road, yield to vehicles driving uphill by using the nearest turnout.

Key events: Blossom and Music Festival, Cañon City, first weekend of May; Donkey Derby Days, Cripple Creek, second weekend of June; Gold Rush Days, Victor, third weekend of July.

Contact: BLM-Royal Gorge Resource Area, 719-269-8500. Cañon City Chamber of Commerce, 800-876-7922, www.canoncitychamber.com. Cripple Creek Welcome Center, 877-858-GOLD.

A network of four north-south roads forms the Gold Belt Tour. Resembling a short-handled pitchfork with three prongs, the byway traverses diverse mountain and meadow landscapes, which create driving experiences ranging from white-knuckle to serene. Depending on the segment, travelers cruise through vast ranchlands, wind through craggy canyons or creep along rock ledges chiseled from steep cliffs. Drivers can choose to explore individual roads or the entire byway.

Starting in the town of Florissant, the

131-mile route heads south on Teller One—the pitchfork handle—and courses through Florissant Fossil Beds National Monument. More than 35 million years ago, volcanic mudflows preserved tens of thousands of plant and insect fossils. Specimens in the visitor center display astounding detail of ancient leaves, beetles and dragonflies. Outside, a nature trail winds past huge fossilized tree stumps.

About 12 miles south, the byway splits into the prongs—High Park, Phantom Canyon and Shelf Roads.

High Park Road veers southwest across mountain meadows flanked with stands of ponderosa pine. In the distance, the snow-crested Sangre de Cristo Range rises from the plains. Ranchers homesteaded this area long before prospectors plied the trail during the 1890s gold boom.

The two-lane paved highway offers a fast and relaxing means to traverse the distance between Cripple Creek and Cañon City. In comparison, the byway's two other segments boast adventurous drives through craggy chasms.

Built atop the rail bed of the former Florence & Cripple Creek Railroad, Phantom Canyon Road branches southeast, paralleling Eightmile Creek. Steam-powered trains hauled gold valued today at $6 billion from 19th-century mining camps to Florence's ore reduction mills. On Sundays, excursion trains transported shoppers to opulent Cripple Creek and picnickers to the fragrant orchards of the Arkansas Valley. A curved steel bridge and two tunnels through solid granite attest to the extraordinary construction feats necessary to build the railway.

As the unpaved route descends 5,000 feet, it hugs sheer pink walls of Pikes Peak granite. Stands of Engelmann spruce and subalpine fir give way to lower-elevation forests of ponderosa pine and Douglas fir. Cottonwoods and willows fringe the creek. After 25 miles of curves, the road opens onto a broad valley dotted with piñon pine and juniper woodlands before entering Florence.

From there, travelers can access Shelf Road—the center prong—by driving northwest to Cañon City. Heading due north to Cripple Creek, this segment passes through the Garden Park Fossil Area, where in 1877 a school superintendent stumbled upon several huge dinosaur fragments, including a 5-foot-long femur. Paleontologists later uncovered an amazing number of massive, nearly complete skeletons of stegosaurus, tyrannosaurus and other dinosaurs in a band of shale measuring only 3 feet thick. Specimens exhumed from this area are displayed in museums around the world, including the Smithsonian and the Denver Museum of Nature & Science.

The asphalt byway then courses through expansive ranch lands. Brilliant white and red strata streak the slopes of the mountains rising

to each side. Towering 100 feet high, rock spires mark Red Canyon Park. A rough road winds to picnic sites nestled among striking sandstone formations.

From this point on, the surface is gravel. After passing the Shelf Rock Climbing Area, the route enters a gorge with limestone-capped granite walls and reaches the lofty section after which it is named—The Shelf. Two hundred feet below, a historic toll collector's cabin still stands on the valley floor. When stagecoaches rumbled through here more than a century ago, the uphill ride took six hours and required three teams of horses.

Vehicles inch along the rock ledge. Although traffic is two-way, this 5-mile stretch is only one lane wide, with occasional turnouts. Four-wheel-drive is recommended and may be required when the surface is wet. Of necessity, motorists miss out on the view. For passengers who keep their eyes open, a dramatic vista of soaring rock walls, sheer drop-offs and a cascading creek unfolds.

The road then corkscrews up a steep canyon sculpted by the waters of Cripple Creek. Eroded by wind and water, Window Rock frames a

patch of sky. Piles of talus stud surrounding slopes, marking old entrances to some of the 500 mines that catacomb the area. Using modern strip mining and heap-leaching technology, today's mining activity focuses on removing and concentrating gold from the waste rock of abandoned mines. To the northeast, majestic Mount Pisgah and Pikes Peak jut into the sky.

At Shelf Road's northern terminus, the city of Cripple Creek, travelers can choose to continue on the Gold Belt Tour or explore this former boomtown. Strolling its quaint streets calms one's nerves after teetering on top of the world.

Ancient Stumps and Bugs

Some 35 million years ago, fiery volcanoes spewed ash into a lake, burying hundreds of thousands of insects, plants, fish, birds and mammals. Today the ancient site is a beautiful mountain valley that cradles Florissant Fossil Beds National Monument. In the beds of shale, insects predominate. Scientists have found species from dragonflies to beetles, including almost all of the known butterflies of the Western hemisphere and four types of tsetse flies, which today exist only in tropical Africa. The volcanic action also petrified sequoia trees. Scores of their stumps stud the grounds. The largest, nicknamed "Big Stump," measures 12 feet high and 38 feet in circumference. Experts estimate that the sequoia once stood 300 feet tall. The Florissant Valley fossil deposit was incredibly rich. When paleontologist Samuel H. Scudder evaluated it in 1877, he and his assistants reportedly unearthed 5,000 specimens in

Photographs, left to right:
1. Mine ruins outside Victor
2. Strip mines extract gold ore.
3. Historic Cripple Creek
4. The Shelf challenges drivers.

five days. More than 50,000 of its fossils reside in museums throughout the world. And, before the site's designation as a national monument, countless others were extracted by vandals and souvenir hunters. In the 1880s, for example, excursion trains scheduled stops at Florissant so passengers could hunt for fossils. Vandals futilely attempted to cart off the "Big Stump," leaving their broken saw blades imbedded in the petrified wood. The excavated fossils that remain are impressive to behold. On the guided Petrified Forest Loop Trail, visitors can view several huge sequoia stumps. Inside the visitor center, a wall exhibit displays 201 delicate fossils. The specimens reveal remarkable detail, such as intricate veins on tree leaves, tiny hairs on wasp legs and even the spots on butterfly wings. [On Teller County Road 1, two miles south of Florissant; 719-748-3253; fee; open year-round.]

Formation of the Garden of the Gods

Eons of erosion sculpted the Garden of the Gods' fascinating spires, towers and balanced rocks. Some 300 million years ago, rubble worn away from the Ancestral Rockies spread in huge alluvial fans over the present-day Colorado Springs area. Wind and sun eventually dried them into sandstone and mud-stone conglomerates. The uplift of the modern Rockies, which began about 60 million years ago, activated the Rampart Range Fault on which the garden is located. Sedimentary rock lying horizontally on the fault swelled upward, then fractured and tilted. During subsequent millennia, additional cycles of uplift and erosion chiseled the landscape, creating such whimsical formations as the Tower of Babel and Kissing Camels.

[Garden of the Gods Visitor Center, 1805 N. 30th St., Colorado Springs; 719-634-6666; free; open year-round.]

Cripple Creek

Travelers still come to Cripple Creek in hopes of striking it rich. But today, instead of veins of gold, casinos attract them. Stately Victorian buildings dating from the former mining camp's bonanza years line Bennett Avenue. Besides limited stakes gambling enterprises, they house restaurants, shops and quaint hotels. Even in the 21st century, wild donkeys still roam the streets.

Activities abound. In the summertime, audiences hiss at villains during Butte Opera House melodramas. The Cripple Creek & Victor steam-powered train chugs on narrow-gauge tracks through the mining district. At the Mollie Kathleen Gold Mine, adventurous visitors ride in a nine-man cage 1,000 feet down into its depths.

Photographs this page:
1. Petrified sequoia tree stump
2. Gateway rocks at Garden of the Gods

Frontier Pathways

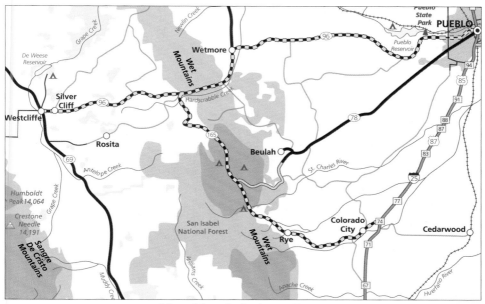

Map of Frontier Pathways Byway

The towering peaks of the Sangre de Cristo Range, hardy old-growth forests of the Wet Mountains and numerous vintage homesteads distinguish the Frontier Pathways byway.

Shaped like a wishbone, the 103-mile route arcs between Pueblo and Colorado City, with a

Photographs this page:
1. Lover's Leap at Hardscrabble Canyon
2. Historic Beckwith Ranch near Westcliffe

spur extending to Westcliffe.

From its southern gateway at the planned development of Colorado City, the route heads west across the plains of Greenhorn Valley. Translated from Spanish, the name honors Cuerño Verde, chief of the Comanches who once roamed these lands. After passing by cattle ranches, the road traverses the quiet village of Rye, once known for its dairies and sawmills.

In the early 1960s, Colorado greenback cutthroat trout, which were thought to be extinct, were discovered in a small stream near Rye. Successful recovery efforts led to reintroduction

Trip Planner: Frontier Pathways

Route: Follows Colorado 96 west from Pueblo to Westcliffe and turns on Colorado 165 southeast to Colorado City.
Total length: 103 miles.
Driving time: Three and one-half hours, excluding stops.
Outstanding features: Wet Mountains, San-gre de Cristo Range, abundance of original homesteads.
Vehicle restrictions: None.
Accessibility: Year-round.
Key events: Chiles and Frijoles Festival, Pueblo, third weekend of September; Wet Mountain Western Days Music and Arts Festi-val, Westcliffe, Labor Day Weekend.
Contact: El Pueblo Museum, 719-583-0453. Chambers of Commerce: Greater Pueblo, 800-233-3446, www.pueblochamber.org; Westcliffe, 877-793-3170, www.custercountyco.com

of this native species into Arkansas and South Platte river drainages. As a result, its status improved from endangered to threatened. The greenback cutthroat trout is Colorado's official fish.

Scrub oaks and piñon pines dapple the landscape before the road turns northwest into the San Isabel National Forest. Recreational options within the forest abound: camping, hiking, backpacking, motorcycling, mountain biking, horseback riding, kayaking and rafting. Lake Isabel, formed in the 1930s when Civilian Conservation Corps workers built the dam, shimmers among spruce and fir trees. Anglers and boaters gravitate to its calm water.

Flanked with dark, dense old-growth forests, the Wet Mountains rise to the west. The area's moist climate often envelopes the byway in mist. Within this sublime setting, the quixotic

one-man building project known as the Bishop Castle continues to take shape. Native rock towers and buttresses stir travelers' curiosity.

As the road leaves the national forest, it climbs over 9,400-foot Bigelow Divide, and then 9,379-foot Wixson Divide. The weathered wood structures of several original homesteads still stand in the high mountain meadows. Among them is the Drake homestead, whose owner not only ranched but also operated a post office from the front room of his house. Ponderosa pines, Douglas firs and aspens scale the surrounding slopes.

At McKenzie Junction, the byway turns west along the base of the "wishbone." A stunning panorama of the jagged, snow-capped Sangre de Cristo Range evokes awe. In this 50-mile stretch of the range, 22 peaks tower more than 13,000 feet high. An expansive valley stretches to the foothills. Sagebrush and rabbitbrush tuft the arid terrain. Many of the ranches date to the 1840s.

Silver and gold ore discovered in the 1870s

caused Rosita, Silver Cliff and other towns to sprout throughout the valley. Once the boom subsided, they withered like drought-stricken wildflowers. In contrast, the site chosen as the Denver and Rio Grande Railroad's terminal, Westcliffe, flourished.

Quaint western buildings housing galleries, shops and restaurants line its broad main street. Inside the century-old Westcliff Schoolhouse, its name confusingly spelled without a final "e," a museum chronicles the area's history. The community hosts entertaining events ranging from craft fairs to rodeos, theater and jazz festivals.

From Westcliffe, the byway backtracks across the valley to McKenzie Junction and into the Wet Mountains and San Isabel National Forest. Tall stands of healthy blue spruce hug the slopes. Rugged granite walls striped with bands of gneiss squeeze Hardscrabble Canyon into a narrow passage.

The 19th-century town of Wetmore guards the eastern mouth of the canyon. Earlier settlements in the area, such as Buzzard's Roost, served as posts where French fur trappers traded with Ute Indians.

Photographs, left to right:
1. Sangre de Cristo Range and Wet Mountain Valley
2. Ranch in Wet Mountain Valley
3. Golden eagle at Raptor Center of Pueblo
4. General store in Wetmore

The byway descends into foothills carpeted with scrub-oak woodlands. Stagecoaches carrying passengers from Pueblo to Wet Mountain Valley mining towns once joggled along this route. Old weathered stage stop buildings still stand atop Jackson Hill.

As the road continues east, piñon pines and juniper trees speckle the sere plains. The rippling water of 11-mile-long Lake Pueblo glistens on the flat terrain. Visitors to Lake Pueblo State Park can boat, fish, swim, water ski and picnic.

A few miles farther, the byway reaches its northern terminus, Pueblo. Originally founded as a trading post, this prairie community has seen countless trappers, traders, fortune seekers and pioneers etch paths westward.

Catch and Release

The purpose of catch and release is to improve fishing by solving problems peculiar to specific waters, such as low spawning success and low survival rates of young trout. This regulation helps greenback cutthroat trout and other unique species reproduce and increase their population density. Anglers who hook a catch-and-release fish can increase its chance of survival by doing the following: reel in the fish quickly; keep the fish in the water while handling it or the hook; remove the hook gently; if the hook cannot be removed gently, cut the line as close to the hook as possible; gently hold the fish upright and move it back and forth in the water to help it regain its equilibrium. For anglers, the catch and release regulation provides the exhilarating experience of fishing in waters filled with large numbers of sizeable specimens.

A Haven for Birds of Prey

On a wide bend of the meandering Arkansas River, the Greenway & Nature Center of Pueblo harbors wounded birds of prey in its raptor center. The goal of the Raptor Center of Pueblo is to restore the birds to health and release them into the wild. Annually, 300 injured eagles, hawks, owls and falcons receive convalescent care in the rehabilitation area. Of these about half return to their home environment. Twenty or so "educator" birds, which due to irreparable injuries or human imprint can never be released, are on display for visitors to view. A barn owl named Skyler, for example, has no understanding of bird of prey behavior because individuals took it out of its environment when it was only a chick. Due to this human imprint, it would not survive in the wild. Other facilities include the Max Watt Interpretive Center, which features exhibits about water-focused subjects, a fishing deck, Xeriscape gardens, playground, gift shop, picnic areas and a riverside restaurant. In addition, from here visitors can access more than 21 miles of paved trails along the Arkansas River and Fountain Creek.

[5200 Nature Center Road, Pueblo; Nature Center, 719-549-2414; Raptor Center, 719-549-2327; free; open year-round.]

Pueblo

Located on the confluence of Fountain Creek and the Arkansas River, Pueblo features several river-focused attractions. Paintings along the Arkansas River Levee form, according to Guiness, the "world's largest mural." The Arkansas River Walk invites strollers to enjoy the urban waterfront. In the Union Avenue Historic District many of the street's grand buildings have been restored to their original splendor. The Pueblo Union Depot, complete with stained glass windows, burnished wood wainscoting and mosaic tile floors, exhibits works by area artists. The historic boathouse in Mineral Palace Park also displays local artists' creations.

The city celebrates its history through several museums. Built on the original trading post site, El Pueblo Museum presents the area's rich multi-cultural heritage. Rosemount Museum showcases the residence of John A. Thatcher, a cattle, mining and agriculture baron. Other interesting collections include planes and jets of different eras at the Fred E. Weisbrod/International B-24 Memorial Museum and fire fighting equipment in the Hose Company No. 3 Fire Museum.

In City Park, visitors can ride on a restored 1911 Parker carousel or observe hundreds of animals exhibited in naturalistic settings at the Pueblo Zoo.

A 35-mile trail starting at the University of Southern Colorado stretches to Lake Pueblo, popular for water sports and picnics. On the way is the Greenway & Nature Center of Pueblo. The Raptor Center is the main attraction of this educational and recreational facility.

Photographs this page:
1. The Clarkson homestead in the Wet Mountains
2. Winter sunrise on the Sangre de Cristo Range

Highway of Legends

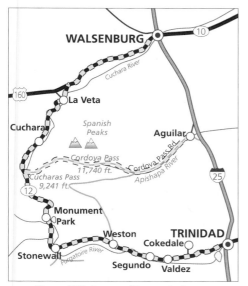

WALSENBURG

La Veta

Cuchara

Spanish Peaks

Aguilar

Cordova Pass
11,740 ft.

Cordova Pass Rd.

Cucharas Pass
9,241 ft.

Apishapa River

Cuchara River

Monument Park

Weston

Cokedale

TRINIDAD

Stonewall

Purgatoire River

Segundo

Valdez

Map of Highway of Legends Byway

Trip Planner: Highway of Legends

Route: Follows Colorado 12 between Walsenburg and Trinidad. Passes through the Cucharas and Purgatoire river valleys, into the San Isabel National Forest and over Cucharas Pass. An addition designated in 2002, Cordova Pass Road, links Cucharas Pass with Aguilar on Interstate 25 via Cordova Pass.
Total length: 82 miles.
Driving time: Two hours, excluding stops.
Outstanding features: Spanish Peaks, dikes and other unusual geological formations, Cucharas Pass, Native American and Hispanic legends, quaint coal-mining towns and Hispanic settlements.
Vehicle restrictions: None.
Accessibility: Open year-round.
Key events: Oktoberfest, La Veta and Cuchara, first weekend of October.
Contact: Trinidad Welcome Center, 719-846-9512. Chambers of Commerce: La Veta/Cuchara, 719-742-3676, www.lavetacucharachamber.com; Trinidad, 719-846-9285, www.trinidadco.com; Walsenburg, 719-738-1065.

L ike spokes on a wheel, hundreds of rock walls radiate out from the towering Spanish Peaks. Some thick, others thin, they stretch down the slopes into verdant valleys. Throughout human history, these and other extraordinary features have inspired enchanting tales that spice the Highway of Legends.

Anchored by Walsenburg and Trinidad, the 82-mile byway climbs west from semi-arid plains into lush river valleys and the San Isabel National Forest before cresting at 9,994-foot Cucharas Pass.

The northern gateway, Walsenburg, earned its nickname "The City Built on Coal" in the early 1900s. At that time, the sounds of some 40 languages filled area coal mines and camps. Exhibits in the Walsenburg Mining Museum chronicle that era. Outside of town, water enthusiasts fish and boat on Lathrop State Park's

Photographs this page:
1. Dikes radiate from the Spanish Peaks.
2. Goemmer Butte is a volcanic plug.

two lakes while hikers trek grassland trails.

Piñon pine and juniper woodlands dapple rolling hills framing the Cucharas River Valley. The twin Spanish Peaks tower on the southern horizon. Prehistoric Indians named them Huajatolla, meaning the "Breasts of the Earth" or wellspring of life.

The highway turns south to La Veta, which nestles below the bald, gray mountaintops. Established in the 1860s as a trading post, the community now thrives on ranching and the arts. Several impressive galleries showcase local artists' creations. Visitors can explore life in the early years by touring the Fort Francisco Museum.

As the road continues, odd geological formations capture travelers' attention. Goemmer's Butte, a 500-foot-high volcanic plug, thrusts up from the valley floor like a sore thumb.

Profile Rock teases viewers to discern images of George Washington and Thomas Jefferson in its curves and crevasses. This prominent landmark is one of the area's hundreds of dikes. Created by volcanic action, these unique walls radiate down from the peaks.

Some, like the Devil's Stairsteps, have inspired legends. Its silhouette indeed looks like a set of steps stretching up the slope. According to lore, eons ago the devil left his fiery abode to survey the world. He climbed the steps to the top of the Spanish Peaks, admired what he saw and began plotting to seize the mountains and valleys. When God learned of his plans, he claimed the area as his own and forbade the devil from entering Cucharas Valley ever again.

Dense fir and spruce forests replace scruboak woodlands as the road winds upwards. After passing through a gap in towering Dakota Wall, the byway reaches Cuchara. The town's economic base evolved from potato growing and cheesemaking to mountain resort activities enhanced by San Isabel National Forest. Village shops offer antiques, handcrafted goods and gifts.

Stands of aspen beautify 9,941-foot-high Cucharas Pass. In autumn, their golden hue dribbles down the slopes like honey. West Spanish Peak fills the scene with its stately pyramid shape. Mid-June through late July, perky blossoms dapple the mountain meadow viewed from the John B. Farley Wildflower Overlook.

In 2002, Cordova Pass Road, which connects Cucharas Pass to the town of Aguilar (near Interstate 25) via Cordova Pass, was added to the Highway of Legends. From Cucharas Pass, a 5-mile segment of this road leads to Vista Point Handicapped Trail. An awe-inspiring panorama rewards those who take the hike. From this 11,000-foot vantage point, several dike "wheel spokes" radiating from the "hub" can be viewed at one time. To the south, a vista of Trinidad, the basalt-capped mesa called Fisher's Peak and New Mexico unfolds.

From here, travelers can return to the main highway or continue on the byway addition for 35 miles to Aguilar. One of the highlights of the latter's unpaved route is Apishapa Arch, a man-made opening through one of the fin-shaped dikes.

As the primary route (Colorado 12) descends from Cucharas Pass, it passes two high altitude lakes cradled in forests. Anglers hook rainbow, cutthroat, kokanee and brown trout in North Lake. According to lore, Monument Lake was created from the tears of two chiefs who cried in

Photographs, left to right:
1. Cordova Pass Road leads to the Spanish Peaks.
2. Coke ovens outside Cokedale
3. Devil's Stairsteps

desperation when they failed to find water for their tribes.

An impressive, 250-foot-high sandstone formation heralds the entrance to the ranching community of Stonewall. From here, the road turns east into the rich farmlands of Purgatoire River Valley. In the 1860s, New Mexican settlers built Cordova Plaza and other quaint Hispanic villages along the river.

Several mining and coking camps sprouted up in this coal-laced region in the early 1900s. The remains of several hundred coking ovens border the byway at the entrance to Cokedale. Their fires once lit up the night sky with a red glow.

Fringed by piñon pine and juniper woodlands, the highway reaches Trinidad State Park. In addition to hiking, boating and fishing, it features a watchable wildlife area. Following a three-quarter-mile nature trail in Long's Canyon, hikers may see mule deer, collared lizards and cottontail rabbits. Wildlife blinds overlook wetlands, making it easier to observe great blue herons and other birds.

The byway's southeastern point ends at Trinidad, a community rich with Hispanic heritage. From here, the high plains stretch endlessly eastward. On the western horizon, though, the slate-gray Spanish Peaks shine like beacons, luring travelers to climb their slopes to shimmering lakes, dense forests and unique rock formations.

Model Coal Camp

Ebony mounds and remains of coking ovens mark the turnoff to Cokedale, once a thriving coal mining camp. Founded in 1906 by the American Smelting and Refining Company, the model camp soon boasted a population of 1,500. More than 350 ovens carbonized the coal output of area mines. Due to decreased demand, the mines closed shortly after World War II. The company offered homes to the townspeople for $100 per room and $50 per lot. Those who stayed incorporated the community in 1948. Listed on the National Register of Historic Places, Cokedale looks much as it did at the turn of the 20th century. Signs identify key buildings such as the former bath house, mercantile store, mining office and superintendent's home. Most of the residents live in tiny, stucco-sided square houses whose four-sloped roofs peak in the center. With a population now totaling less than a tenth of its original size, the quaint community preserves a segment of the coal mining era.

Wondrous Walls

Like spokes of a wheel, more than 400 unique walls, called dikes, radiate down from the Spanish Peaks. These extraordinary geological formations were formed eons ago by volcanic action. Magma seeped into fractures in sedimentary rock and eventually hardened. Over time, erosion wore away the softer material, exposing fin-like shapes. The dikes rise up to 100 feet high and measure from one foot to 100 feet in width. They stretch above or below ground as far as 25 miles. Most prominent are Profile Rock and the Devil's Stairsteps.

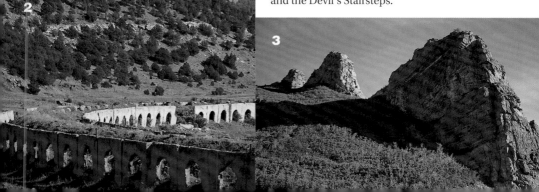

Santa Fe Trail

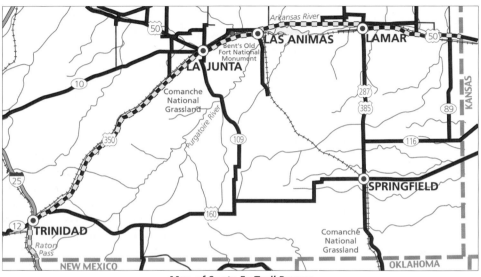

Map of Santa Fe Trail Byway

The semi-arid prairie of southeastern Colorado stretches in all directions, its sun-drenched haze teasing travelers on the Santa Fe Trail byway with mirages. Antelope prong through the grasses. Nesting birds trill. On the western horizon, the Spanish Peaks rise like beacons, signaling the end of the plains.

More than 170 years ago, freight wagons straining under loads of profitable goods indelibly marked the trail as they gouged ruts into the short-grass prairie. Today, a paved national scenic byway follows the legendary, 900-mile commercial route. The 188-mile segment that arcs across southeastern Colorado forms the state's Santa Fe Trail Scenic and Historic Byway.

Known historically as the Mountain Route, this section parallels the Arkansas River from the Kansas border west to La Junta, turns southwest to Trinidad, and then veers south to New Mexico.

The Santa Fe Trail opened to commerce in 1821 when William Becknell of Franklin, Missouri, traded his pack train of merchandise with Santa Fe residents. Freshly independent from Spanish rule that had forbidden trade with foreigners, Santa Feans seized the opportunity to

Trip Planner: Santa Fe Trail

Route: From the Kansas border, it follows U.S. 50 west to La Junta, U.S. 350 to Trinidad and Interstate 25 to the New Mexico border.
Total length: 188 miles.
Driving time: Four hours, excluding stops.
Outstanding features: Prairie landscape, birds, Bent's Old Fort National Historic Site, Comanche National Grassland, Spanish Peaks, Fisher Peak, and Raton Pass.
Vehicle restrictions: None.
Accessibility: Open year-round.
Key events: Santa Fe Trail Festival, Trinidad, first weekend of June; Santa Fe Trail Encampment, Bent's Old Fort National Historic Site, last weekend of July.
Contact: Trinidad/Las Animas Economic Development Inc., 719-846-9412. Chambers of Commerce: La Junta, 719-384-7411, www.lajunta.net; Lamar, 719-336-4379; Las Animas/Bent County, 719-456-0453; Trinidad, 719-846-9285, www.trinidadco.com

barter silver, furs and mules for manufactured goods. Tales of extraordinary profits — reportedly 2,000 percent for Becknell — spread like prairie fire. For the next 59 years, millions of dollars in merchandise traveled east and west on the trail.

In Lamar, near the Colorado byway's eastern terminus, a "Madonna of the Trail" statue honors the route's historic significance. During the trail age, this area was named Big Timbers after the dense groves of cottonwoods growing on both sides of the Arkansas River. Travelers welcomed the trees' shelter from strong winds and summer heat.

For merchants and pioneers heading westward on the Mountain Route, Bent's Fort offered the first way station in nearly 200 miles. Weary travelers nicknamed the adobe haven the "Castle of the Plains."

From 1833 to 1850, the trading post bustled with activity. Laden with beaver pelts and buffalo robes, trappers and hunters swaggered into the trade room to barter for blankets, gunpowder and ironware. Cheyenne, Arapaho and other tribal members held peace talks in the council room. Mexican laborers maintained the property while merchants and pioneers replenished supplies and repaired equipment. Indeed, the site epitomized a cultural as well as commercial crossroads.

Today's travelers can experience life along the trail at Bent's Old Fort National Historic Site, a reconstruction of the original trading post. Costumed interpreters enliven the fort with their animated portrayal of trappers, tradesmen, Mexican cooks and soldiers. In the trade room, a merchant displays wares that include such luxuries as Chinese tea and Italian

Photographs, left to right:
1. Bent's Old Fort National Historic Site
2. Native American re-enactor trains horse.
3. Vogel Canyon in Comanche Grassland
4. Native prairie grasses on Comanche Grassland

beads. The pings of hammer against anvil bounce out of the blacksmith shop. Guided tours reveal the owners' favorite gathering place — a large billiard room overlooking the plaza.

As the byway turns southwest from La Junta, the distant Spanish Peaks rise into view. Just off the juncture with Colorado 71, Sierra Vista Overlook presents a sweeping view of the Rocky Mountains and surrounding prairie. Wayfarers who enjoy hiking may want to pack a lunch and trek three miles of the Santa Fe Historic Trail to the Timpas Picnic Area.

The route then traverses the Comanche National Grassland. There, travelers can see areas restored to native grasses predominant before settlement. Besides short-grass prairie, the landscape also contains marshlands and canyons. The diversity of habitats attracts a wide variety of resident and migratory birds. The preserve also contains rock art and the largest documented dinosaur track site.

The Santa Fe Trail coursed through the heart of Trinidad, now known as the Corazón de Trinidad National Historic District. Located in the fertile Purgatoire River Valley, this ranching and farming community thrived on supplying trail traffic. The Trinidad History Museum complex depicts that vibrant period. Its Santa Fe Trail Museum chronicles the lifestyles of the region's early inhabitants through historic photographs, family possessions and commercial goods. The Baca House and Bloom Mansion show the difference in lifestyles during the city's trail and railroad eras.

From Trinidad, freight caravans and covered wagons started the arduous 20-mile climb up Raton Pass. In the late 1860s, enterprising "Uncle Dick" Wootton built a toll road over it, charging 25 cents per wagon and a dime per head of livestock. Although expensive, the improved surface eased the trip considerably.

Caravans inched up Raton Pass at speeds slower than a mile per hour. Completing the final stretch into New Mexico, which takes today's byway travelers mere minutes on the interstate highway, took them as long as a week.

Comanche Grassland

The largest documented dinosaur track site in North America, some 275 species of birds and intriguing prehistoric rock art lure visitors to Comanche Grassland. Interspersed with farm and ranch tracts, the preserve stretches from La Junta to the southeast corner of Colorado.

During the Jurassic Period about 150 million years ago, two types of dinosaurs left their footprints, which later fossilized, in the muddy shoreline of a large shallow lake. The site lies within Picket Wire Canyonlands, 30 miles south of La Junta. Today visitors can see about 100 different trackways containing more than 1,300

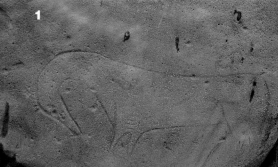

visible impressions. Ferocious, carnivorous allosaurus left 60 percent of the marks, readily identifiable by their three-toed configuration. Enormous, four-footed brontosaurus formed the rest of the footprints. Although these plant-eating dinosaurs weighed around 33 tons, the comparatively small but fierce allosaurus readily preyed upon them. Parallel trackways indicate that the brontosaurus traveled in herds, possibly as protection against predators. Visiting the trackways requires hiking more than 10 miles round trip.

The grassland's diversity of habitats, which range from short-grass prairie to marshlands and canyons, attracts a wide variety of birds. Ring-necked pheasants, great horned owls, golden eagles, roadrunners and numerous others reside there year-round. During spring and fall migrations, birdwatchers spot such waterfowl and shorebirds as great blue herons, white pelicans and trumpeter swans. Birds that breed there include turkey vultures and prairie falcons.

Sandstone walls in Picket Wire Canyonlands, Vogel Canyon, Carrizo Creek and Picture Canyon display prehistoric rock art. Sites contain both petroglyphs, which are chiseled into the stone, and pictographs, which are painted onto the rock. Archaeologists theorize that nomadic hunter-gatherers created the abstract designs and animal figures up to 4,500 years ago.

[1420 East 3rd Street, La Junta 81050, 719-384-2181; free; open year-round.]

Early Hispanic Leaders

Two Hispanic men indelibly shaped the early development of Trinidad and the surrounding region. Felipe Baca [1829-1874] was a founder of the city. Drawn by the fertile soil of the Purgatoire River Valley, in 1862 he and his wife along with a dozen other families migrated from New Mexico to homestead near the river. Baca built an elaborate irrigation system on 400 acres, which yielded bountiful harvests. As a sheep rancher, he introduced modern shearing methods. His flock eventually numbered more than 10,000 head and became the primary source of his wealth. To acquire his residence in the heart of Trinidad, he bartered some 10 tons of wool. Now known as the Baca House, the two-story adobe home is part of the Trinidad History Museum complex (719-846-7217). A wealthy

Photographs, left to right:
1. The Blue Horse, a petroglyph in Picture Canyon
2. Rock formations in Picture Canyon
3. Native grasses in Picket Wire Canyon
4. Pictograph of a deer in Picture Canyon

stockman and legislator, Casimiro Barela [1847-1920] championed Hispanic causes. As one of the 49 delegates to the Colorado Constitutional Convention, he successfully fought to have the new laws printed in Spanish and German as well as English. He served as a state senator for 41 years. During his tenure, the "Perpetual Legislator" promoted better relations between the United States and Mexico and spearheaded legislation that made Colorado the first state to declare Columbus Day a legal holiday.

Cowboy Artist

As a native of the Trinidad area, Western magazine illustrator and landscape painter Arthur Roy Mitchell [1889-1977] grew up among freighters, trappers and cowboys. These colorful characters and his experience as a ranch hand provided him with wagons-full of detail to incorporate into his art. In the 1920s, he studied in New York City under Harvey Dunn, one of the nation's best illustrators and teachers. "Mitch" created more than 160 covers for Western pulp magazines (so-named because of their cheap paper), including "Fourth of July Western Style" for Western Story Magazine and "Driving Off Rustlers" for Far West Stories. Garish colors and simple, hard-hitting subjects that portrayed the gist of the story characterized the covers. In the 1940s, the artist returned to Trinidad, where he painted landscapes, started the first art class at Trinidad State Junior College and fought successfully to preserve and restore historic buildings that now form the Trinidad History Museum. When he died, his personal collection contained more than 250 of his oil paintings and 6,000 of his sketches, plus dozens of works by Harvey Dunn, Harold Von Schmidt, Grant Reynard and other artist friends. Many now hang in the A.R. Mitchell Museum of Western Art.

[150 E. Main Street, Trinidad; 719-846-4224; fee; open May through September.]

Trinidad

Trinidad's multi-cultural heritage permeates the city. A bronze equestrian statue of Kit Carson, famed mountain man, scout and soldier, commands the city's spacious Kit Carson Park. Petroglyphs and other Native American artifacts are featured in the Louden-Henritze Archaeology Museum. The Baca House, part of the Trinidad History Museum complex, captures the lifestyle of Don Felipe Baca, a Hispanic rancher and one of the city founders.

Trappers, traders, pioneers, soldiers, coal miners, ranchers and myriad entrepreneurs traveled down the city's main thoroughfare. Now called the Corazón de Trinidad National Historic District, it preserves the community's rich character as a major Santa Fe Trail stop and livestock ranching center.

Photographs this page:
1. Allosaurus track in Picket Wire Canyon
2. The Purgatoire River attracted settlers to Trinidad.

Index

Authors

As a travel writer/photographer team, Nancy and David Muenker have explored fascinating destinations throughout the world. In their hearts, though, none compares with their home, Colorado.

While they traveled Colorado's scenic and historic byways, their admiration for the state's diverse geology, vegetation, wildlife and cultural heritage grew even greater. Each time Nancy and David drive one of these routes, they greet the trip as a new adventure. With different seasons, times of day and weather conditions, nature ensures that no two journeys are alike.

The team now has a third member — Sonha, a German shorthair pointer/Brittany mix. Eager and energetic, she joins Nancy and David on many of their road trips, often "singing" at the sights.

David, Nancy and Sonha

We dedicate this book to the precious women who inspired and nurtured our creativity: Loma Muenker, Mary Jane Muenker and Shirley Pollock.